Given In Honor of
Carol Latsis

RYE FREE READING ROOM
Escape to the Library

WILD ABOUT GREENS

WILD ABOUT GREENS

125 Delectable Vegan Recipes for Kale, Collards, Arugula, Bok Choy, and other Leafy Veggies Everyone Loves

BY NAVA ATLAS

PHOTOGRAPHS BY SUSAN VOISIN

STERLING
New York

STERLING
New York

An Imprint of Sterling Publishing
387 Park Avenue South
New York, NY 10016

ISBN 978-1-4027-8588-7 (hardcover)
ISBN 978-1-4027-9632-6 (ebook)

Distributed in Canada by Sterling Publishing
C/o Canadian Manda Group, 165 Dufferin Street
Toronto, Ontario, Canada M6K 3H6
Distributed in the United Kingdom by GMC Distribution Services
Castle Place, 166 High Street, Lewes, East Sussex, England BN7 1XU
Distributed in Australia by Capricorn Link (Australia) Pty. Ltd.
P.O. Box 704, Windsor, NSW 2756, Australia

For information about custom editions, special sales, and premium
and corporate purchases, please contact Sterling Special Sales at
800-805-5489 or specialsales@sterlingpublishing.com.

Book Production: gonzalez defino, ny / gonzalezdefino.com

Printed in China

2 4 6 8 10 9 7 5 3 1

www.sterlingpublishing.com

ACKNOWLEDGMENTS

I'd like to thank Josh Atlas, Helen Gutfriend, Ellen Kanner, Harry and Wendy Lipstein, Marie Panesko, Barbara Pollak, Shen J.C. Robinson, and Susan Voisin, who, when it comes to recipes, planted seeds that flourished on these pages. Knowing that I'm prone to tinker with any recipe that crosses my path, I hope you will recognize at least the essence of your worthy contributions.

Special thanks go to: my husband, Harry Chaim Tabak, for planting too much chard in 2009, which directly led to the idea for this book; my son, Evan Atlas, for helping to develop the green juices in this book; Seth Branitz and Jenn Liemer Branitz of Karma Road Organic Vegan Deli (karmaroad.net) in New Paltz, New York, for allowing Evan and me to use their space to concoct juices and make a mess (which we cleaned up); and to Melissa Mandel, who helped me with research on the background information on all the leafy greens.

This is the third time that Susan Voisin, the deservedly renowned talent behind FatFree Vegan Kitchen (fatfreevegan.com), has done the photography for one of my books. Thank you so much, Susan, for recreating my recipes in such a lovely way once again.

Thanks go to Nathalie Lussier of The Raw Foods Witch (rawfoodswitch.com) for her helpful article on the benefits of and differences between green juices and green smoothies.

As always, I'd like to credit my agents and dear friends, Lisa Ekus and Sally Ekus, who keep me so busy that I'm running out of mushy things to say about them. Thank you, Lisa and Sally, for being the most generous and supportive agents ever.

I always save the final word for the editor of any project, as she (as the case is here) is always the unsung heroine of the process. Jennifer Williams has been that heroine for this as well as my previous book, *Vegan Holiday Kitchen*. Thank you, Jennifer, for being such a warmhearted and fun editor, and for making each book the best it can possibly be.

Also by Nava Atlas

Cookbooks

Vegan Holiday Kitchen
Vegan Soups and Hearty Stews for All Seasons
Vegan Express
The Vegetarian Family Cookbook
The Vegetarian 5-Ingredient Gourmet
Pasta East to West
Great American Vegetarian
Vegetarian Express
Vegetarian Celebrations
Vegetariana

Visual nonfiction

The Literary Ladies' Guide to the Writing Life
Secret Recipes for the Modern Wife
Expect the Unexpected When You're Expecting!

CONTENTS

INTRODUCTION

It won't be terrible if all you ever do with a big bunch of kale, collard greens, or chard is to sauté or braise it in olive oil. Your health and well-being will certainly be enhanced if you do little more than toss tender raw spinach, arugula, and watercress into salads. And if the only way that Asian greens make it into your repertoire is when you quickly wilt them into stir-fries, neither you nor the veggies will be any the worse for it. You're still way ahead of anyone who has yet to make eating leafy greens a daily habit.

But why stop there when there's an abundance of easy ways to prepare and enjoy these supremely nourishing, plentiful, and delicious leafy veggies? Whether you stir them into soups and stews or create vitamin-packed juices and smoothies, greens keep the palate open to delight and surprise. You'll be amazed when you discover how delicious fruit smoothies taste with the addition of spinach and how addictive raw kale salads are. You don't need to follow the old rules anymore about boiling big pots of water (losing vitamins and flavor in the process) to easily prepare and enjoy greens. Stir-fried collard ribbons, anyone?

Interest in leafy greens has proliferated in the past few years, along with their availability, in just about every type of market there is—from farm markets, produce stands, and Community Supported Agriculture (CSA) farms to natural foods stores and even the local supermarket. Not long ago, in the dead of winter, I was stunned to see an array of at least a dozen varieties of fresh greens right in my none-too-urbane local supermarket; they were a sight for sore eyes and a weary palate. Most were organic, since apparently many greens are easy to grow that way. Rarely do I see limp, unloved greens languishing in the produce section—conscious consumers are buying up these fresh, leafy beauties before they have a chance to expire.

I've long been a fan of greens, but with the increased availability of a number of varieties, my enthusiasm for this group of veggies is at an all-time high. When I joined a CSA some years ago, greens of all sorts seemed to be one of the most abundant offerings (from the tender spinach of May to the hardy kale of late autumn, harvested after a heavy frost). I was the official CSA newsletter writer, bartering away an obligation to dig in the dirt (which I prefer to avoid) with a steady flow of recipes and tips for enjoying the produce *du jour*. While most of my fellow CSA members loved the bounty of greens, they also wanted more ideas about what to do with them. There was always so much to take home!

Although this book doesn't go into the subject of growing your own greens, it's well known that leafy veggies are a gardener's delight—they're easy to cultivate and are at their most delicious when freshly harvested. Some gardens yield a dual delight— plants with edible roots and leaves. Turnips, beets, and radishes come to mind. I think it's somewhat sad when stores offer only the root without its greens. (The truth is that leaves are far more perishable than the roots.) When you see leafy greens still attached to the root, take full advantage of this double blessing.

A few years ago my husband started a vegetable garden and discovered that, unlike me, he has a major green thumb. The veggies, greens among them, sometimes seemed to flow into my kitchen faster than I could keep up with the harvest. That's why I've also included a guide to freezing greens at the end of this introduction (page 13). As delightful and versatile as leafy veggies can be, you might feel as I did at a certain point—with what I called "the Swiss chard explosion of 2009"—that enough is enough, and rather than giving up the crop to the groundhogs, you'll want to harvest, prepare, freeze, and save it for a winter's day when it will once again be appreciated and savored in all its glory.

WHAT YOU'LL FIND IN THIS BOOK

For the most part, the focus in these pages is on the most commonly used dark leafy greens, excluding lettuces and ordinary cabbages. I've also opted not to include salad greens like radicchio and Belgian endive (though they do appear in a few recipes), since most cooks are familiar enough with these vegetables and their common uses.

I myself am vegan, and the recipes in this book are completely plant-based. What you add to these flexible recipes, and what you serve them with, is up to you. It's quite fitting to give this plant-focused book a plant-based orientation, since many of these greens are among the richest sources of readily absorbable calcium—a boon to vegans as well as anyone who avoids dairy for other reasons. (There's much more on this topic in the section The Health Benefits of Leafy Greens on page 11.)

At the end of this general introduction is a special section entitled An Introduction to Leafy Greens (pages 16–33), in which I describe the various greens covered in the book and list the recipes that use each. (The recipes themselves, beginning with chapter 1, are organized according to how they're prepared—that is, whether the recipe is for a soup, stew, salad, or smoothie. You'll find the usual suspects in this collection—pastas, stir-fries, and grain and bean dishes.) The organization of the overview section highlights the flexibility and interchangeability of many of the greens. You may come home with a big batch of chard one week and a big batch of kale the next, and there are many recipes that will work for both. The same idea works for spinach and chard, or spinach and arugula. All Asian greens cook down very quickly, and some can be eaten raw; their flavors aren't so dramatically different from one another that they can't be easily interchanged.

There is less emphasis in this book on Asian greens, since many of them simply aren't available to many of us who don't live in major urban areas. As a result, I've focused on the reality of what's available in most markets and gardens. Whether you shop at the supermarket or a farmers' market, you're going to bring home a lot more chard and kale than tatsoi or mizuna.

My passion for greens is constant and never wanes. I used to say that when we ran out of broccoli, it was time to go food shopping. Now that sentiment refers to all kinds of leafy greens. In my opinion, it's a barren fridge that holds no kale, collards, or spinach, and once you make these great veggies staples in your home, I have no doubt you'll feel the same.

THE HEALTH BENEFITS OF LEAFY GREENS

When it comes to nutrition, leafy greens often top lists of the most nutritious veggies, and for good reason. These green wonders offer numerous benefits, including these:

➥ Leafy greens are good sources of vitamins, notably folic acid (a B vitamin), vitamin A, and vitamin C. They're a particularly notable source of vitamin K, which is essential to good bone health.

➥ They're also a rich source of minerals, including potassium, magnesium, and iron.

➥ The calcium content in some leafy greens, especially kale, collard greens, and spinach, is significant. The calcium is also highly absorbable, unlike that in other foods. Thus, for vegans and those who don't consume dairy calcium for other reasons, dark leafy greens can become an important and reliable source for this mineral.

➥ Greens contain large amounts of phytochemicals with antioxidant properties. Carotenoids play a role in protecting the eyes; they and flavonoids like quercetin have been shown to protect against certain cancers.

➥ Other benefits common to many greens is that they're anti-inflammatory; they can also help control blood pressure and help detoxify the body and regulate blood sugar.

➥ A number of greens—notably kale, collards, spinach, chard, and mustard greens—are modest but reliable sources of valuable omega-3 fatty acids.

➥ Greens are high in fiber and quite low in calories and carbohydrates, which makes them great for the digestive tract and for weight maintenance.

➥ Leafy greens are a great source of chlorophyll—the pigment that makes leaves green. It confers all manner of health benefits, including overall support for our internal systems. Many claims are made for chlorophyll's ability to reverse or allay the effects of aging. Chlorophyll is most available in raw greens, which is why their concentration in green smoothies and especially in juices is so valuable.

BUYING & PREPARATION TIPS

Buying

It's best to buy greens the same day you plan to use them or at most the day before. Choose greens with firm, uniform-colored leaves and few, if any, wilted or discolored ones. The more delicate the greens, the more perishable they are. Hardier greens keep well for several days in the refrigerator, but the sooner you use them after they've been harvested, the higher their level of intact nutrients and the better their flavor will be. Wrap fresh greens in paper towels to absorb any extra moisture, and store them in the refrigerator in a tightly sealed plastic bag until you're ready to use them.

Rinsing

The sandy soil in which green leafy vegetables grow tends to cling to the leaves. Nothing ruins a good dish like a mouthful of sand, so be sure to wash leaves very carefully. Greens bought from the supermarket may look much cleaner than the ones you get from a farmers' market or CSA farm, but don't skip the step of giving them a good rinse, even if they're organic and look perfectly clean. You just never know.

If the greens you've purchased from the supermarket—baby spinach, chard, and collard greens, for example—look fairly clean, a good rinse in a colander will suffice. For greens that have more savoyed (the fancy way to say "crinkled") leaves and most Asian greens, the best way to get them really clean is to chop them first, then immerse the leaves in a big bowl of cold water. Swish them around with your hands, then let them stand for a couple of minutes. Scoop out the chopped greens, discard the water, and repeat until the water looks perfectly clean. Even after doing this, I'm not content until I give the greens a final rinse in a colander.

Stemming & Chopping

To use stems, or not? That's a matter of personal preference for each cook. Small greens like baby spinach, arugula, and tatsoi need not be stemmed at all. The stem, or midrib, of mustard greens is tender and can be chopped or sliced along with the leaf. Stems of larger spinach and arugula leaves tend to be stringy, and I like to remove them, though other cooks may not find them bothersome.

For all varieties of kale and chard, it's best to cut or tear the leaves away from the stems; then if you'd like to use them, slice the stems very thinly. I like chard stems; they're kind of celery-like in texture, and rainbow chard stems look decorative in most dishes. I can take or leave kale stems; I don't find they add or detract much from any preparation, so whether they end up in the finished dish or in the compost is largely a matter of my mood. Chard and kale, thus stemmed, can be sliced into ribbons or chopped into bite-size pieces. It's easier to cut flatter leaves of chard and lacinato kale into nice ribbons, but it's fairly pointless to try to cut the leaves of curly kale that way. Curly kale leaves bounce all over the place while you're trying to cut them, so chopping into bite-size pieces any which way works best.

Collard green stems are too bitter and tough for my taste, so off to the compost they go. My favorite way to cut collard leaves is to stack six or so similar-size halves of leaves, roll them up snugly from one of the narrow ends, then slice thinly. Once they're nicely cut into these long, narrow ribbons, chop them in several places to shorten them. For me, this method of cutting collards has supplanted the older one of boiling the whole leaves for 15 to 20 minutes, then chopping.

FREEZING GREENS

The freezing methods outlined below are for anyone who has a garden that produces an overabundance of greens or belongs to a CSA that offers more greens in a weekly share than anyone can possibly use. If I had learned and practiced these techniques during the Swiss chard explosion of 2009, I wouldn't have been so unhappy whenever my husband came in with yet another bushel of the stuff.

Freezing works particularly well for hardy greens, and is a good way to store spinach and arugula as well, but is not ideal for delicate Asian greens or watercress. Blanching is the more traditional method of preparation for freezing greens. Here are the basic steps for blanching:

1. Stem, chop, and wash greens very well. Bring a pot of water to a boil (the pot should be large enough to accommodate the greens comfortably).

2. Prepare a large bowl of very cold water.

3. Once the water is at a boil, immerse the greens into the water quickly. Cook briefly, depending on the type of greens (30 seconds or so for tender greens like spinach and arugula; 2 to 3 minutes for collard greens; and somewhere in between for kale, chard, mustard greens, broccoli rabe, and Asian greens), just until the leaves are bright green and barely tender.

4. Drain the greens and plunge them into the cold water to stop the cooking process. Drain well again.

5. Pack the greens into small containers, with as little air as possible, or into freezer bags. Push out the excess air and freeze them at once—after, if you like, affixing a label with the date.

A more contemporary method is to stir-fry clean, chopped greens, using as little oil as possible (and including chopped garlic, if you want), until they are tender-crisp. Let the greens cool uncovered, then pack and freeze them, as in step 5 above. Allow the greens to thaw in the refrigerator, or let them thaw partially before adding them to stews or soups. Frozen greens are best used within six months of preparation.

DEHYDRATING GREENS

'll come right out and say it—I don't think dehydration is a good method for preserving greens. When I experimented with it, my feeling was that reducing juicy greens to dried chips, with the idea of rehydrating them at some point, was too much work for the results. Because an average-size dehydrator can hold just so much, drying a big batch of greens can be a huge undertaking. And because the leaves curl this way and that, this method doesn't even offer the space-saving advantage that freezing does.

However, dehydrating does offer an alternative to the oven for making small batches of green chips. Slow drying in a dehydrator most likely preserves more nutrients in the leaves, and they dry more evenly than they do in the oven. The best greens to use in a dehydrator are curly kale and collard greens. Baby spinach works well, too, and needs little preparation.

Using a Dehydrator

To get started, cut clean kale or collard leaves into bite-size pieces. Make sure they're already dry before you put them into a dehydrator. You can toss them with a little oil and salt; for added flavor, experiment with your favorite spices as well as some nutritional yeast.

Each dehydrator is a little different, but as a starting point, try drying baby spinach at 110°F for 6 to 8 hours or kale and collards at 130°F for 8 to 10 hours. Once the leaves feel dry and crispy, dehydrate them for yet a little longer. The greens don't stay nice and crisp unless they're completely dried.

It's best to eat these chips as soon as they're done, since they taste best fresh from the dehydrator. Crisp greens absorb moisture from the air and become less crisp the longer they stand. If you don't finish this addictive snack at once, store any dried green chips in an airtight container. Use them as soon as possible, since for all intents and purposes they are still fresh veggies. During warm months, store them in the refrigerator.

AN INTRODUCTION TO LEAFY GREENS

Finally, on to the different types of greens: how best to enjoy them and where you'll find them in this book. To maximize the interchangeability of recipes in terms of using various ingredients, the book is arranged into chapters according to recipe type rather than the type of green. This section, on the other hand, is organized by type of green and tells you where you can find recipes or basic preparations for each. That way, if you come home from your CSA (Community Supported Agriculture) farm with a big bunch of mustard greens, you can zero in on it in this alphabetical list, rather than search for it in the chapters or the index.

The types of greens you'll find here are the more commonly available varieties as well as those that tend to come in big batches just begging for lots of ideas and uses. Thus, the lists of recipes for arugula, spinach, and kale, for instance, will be much longer than those for radish greens, dandelion greens, or mizuna.

ARUGULA

Long considered a "gourmet" food, arugula is a member of the cruciferous vegetable family. A cool-weather green, it first appears in early spring, with a follow-up in the fall, when it grows late into the season. Arugula's bold but not bitter taste is sometimes described as peppery or mustardy, although somehow these words fail to capture its unique quality. Maybe this flavorful green would seem less precious if we Americans called it by its European names—rocket or rocket salad. Baby or young arugula leaves are less pungent than leaves that are left to grow larger before harvesting. Arugula is used raw (in which form it retains more of its bite) and wilted or very lightly cooked.

Though its flavor is more assertive, arugula is similar to spinach in the ways it can be used, and it can be interchanged with spinach in many dishes. Beyond the formal recipes listed below, you can use it by simply tossing some into your green salad improvisations (it mixes well with tender lettuces like Boston or Bibb), including it in sandwiches in place of lettuce, or wilting some on pizza hot out of the oven.

ASIAN GREENS

I've excluded both the large and baby varieties of bok choy from this section of
the book since these greens have become so readily available they're classified on
their own. The same goes for tatsoi and mizuna, Japanese greens that are more
commonly offered by farmers' markets and CSA farms than other Asian greens
discussed here.

What I generally refer to as "Asian greens" include many varieties that include
the word "choy" in their name—dai gai choy (Chinese mustard cabbage), tung choy
(water spinach), and choy sum (Chinese flowering cabbage). Quite a few of these
greens consist of an edible stalk and tender leaves, both of which cook down quickly
in stir-fries and soups. To my novice palate, many of these greens have a similar
taste—slightly sweet and mildly peppery.

The usual drill—giving all greens a thorough wash before eating them—
applies to Asian greens. A lovely bunch of choys I brought home from a Chinatown
produce stand in New York City was spoiled by my lack of diligence. Although the
greens didn't look particularly muddy, simply rinsing them wasn't sufficient to remove
all the sand that was trapped in the small crevices where leaves and stems meet.

I highly recommend roughly chopping greens before washing them. For greens other than Chinese broccoli (gai lan) and some of the choys, whose stems you actually eat as well as the leaves (don't worry, the difference is easy to tell), you should get rid of the tough midribs, which can be bitter and stringy. For greens with edible stems, trim off about an inch from the bottom, and cut the remaining stem into approximately 2- to 3-inch segments, leaves and all. Then follow the instructions for thoroughly washing greens on page 12.

Most Asian greens can be used raw in salads when they're very small and young, but for the most part these greens will find most favor (to the Western palate) in simple stir-fries and Asian-style soups. The exception to this is bok choy (both the regular and baby varieties), which is always just as good raw as it is lightly stir-fried or braised.

Asian Greens in Basic Preparations
Wine & Mustard–Braised Asian Greens, page 60
Basic Stir-Fried Asian Greens, page 68

Asian Greens with Beans, Grains, Pasta & Other Vegetables
Pad See Ew (Thai Rice Noodles with Chinese Broccoli), page 122

Asian Greens in Soups & Stews
Asian Noodle Soup with Greens & Shiitake Mushrooms, page 144 ✍ Hot-and-Sour Vegetable Soup with Asian Greens, page 196

Choy Sum

Chinese Mustard Cabbage

Chinese Broccoli

BEET GREENS

Unless they grow prolifically in your home garden, a typical bunch of beets bought in a store consists of three to five beets and a modest amount of greens. In terms of flavor and texture, the greens are comparable to chard and can have a slightly salty undertone. Greens from beets of different colors taste fairly similar.

There's no reason not to use raw beet greens, but they're somewhat less palatable that way—light cooking brings out their flavor while reducing a less than pleasing chewiness. Big bunches of beet greens are rare, and a typical bunch wilts down to quite a modest amount. That's why I've included so few recipes for beet greens. In a couple of instances I've included them in dishes along with the beets, and in others I've suggested adding to dishes that include other kinds of greens. For juices that call for beets, the greens are a wonderful addition.

If you find yourself with an abundance of beet greens, you can use them in place of or in addition to chard or spinach in recipes that feature those greens in a lightly cooked form. As with chard, whether or not to use the thinly sliced stems (those from red beets "bleed" quite a bit) is up to the individual cook.

BOK CHOY

Of all Asian greens, bok choy is arguably the most widely known and available. In this book, the term "bok choy" is used somewhat generically to describe the larger variety of this versatile green, with its crisp white stalks and dark leaves. Baby bok choy is a smaller version of this variety that can easily be recognized by the fairly uniform pale green hue of its stems and leaves. I always think of bok choy as a two-for-the-price-of-one item: a crisp veggie plus leafy greens—all in one neat package.

Most people who enjoy eating a wide variety of greens at home or who have eaten them in Chinese restaurants are likely to have been exposed to this mild, easy-to-like vegetable. In Asia, however, there are at least twenty varieties of this versatile green that are consumed with more frequency than the varieties available in the United States. If you scour Asian markets, you might find a variety of bok choy that's half the size of the baby bok choy commonly found in most U.S. markets. If you're lucky enough to come across it, you can simply use it whole in stir-fries.

No matter what the variety, bok choy is equally good raw, in salads, or very lightly cooked in stir-fries and Asian-style soups. To prepare bok choy, just trim an inch or so off the bottom of the stem (if it's a larger stalk) and slice the whole plant, leaves and all. Seared Baby Bok Choy (page 75) is a deliciously different (and completely minimalist) preparation, in which all you do is cut the vegetable in half and brown it in a pan. Delicious.

Bok Choy in Basic Preparations

Bok Choy with Beans, Grains, Pasta & Other Vegetables

BROCCOLI RABE

This leafy vegetable, so popular in Mediterranean cuisine,
is known by many names, including rapini and Italian
broccoli. Despite its name, broccoli rabe is actually a
relative of turnips and mustard greens, not common broccoli.
Its leafy clusters of dark green leaves, narrow stalks, and
tiny, broccoli-like florets are all edible. While some recipes
suggest cooking the stalks before adding the leaves and florets,
I simply cut the stalks into narrow segments and toss them
into the pan, pot, or whatever I'm using, along with the rest
of the plant.

To temper the fairly mild bitterness of this versatile
green, broccoli rabe can be blanched (page 38), but for those
who love the flavor just as it is, in all its bitter glory, broccoli
rabe can be eaten or deliciously showcased in simple sautés.
In most recipes it can be substituted for escarole.

CHARD

At one time this abundant garden vegetable, a relative of both beets and spinach, was generically referred to as Swiss chard. There are a number of varieties of this green, and I refer to them throughout this book simply as chard. In recipes that call for chard, any variety can be used. Some common types of chard besides Swiss chard are green, red, gold, and silver beet chard. "Rainbow chard" is actually five colors of silver beet greens, which grow in a variety of stem colors, packaged together to create a rainbow of colors.

The slight bitterness of chard, with its undertone of saltiness, can be tempered by light cooking, a bit longer than spinach, but a deft touch is in order—you don't want to cook this sprightly green into a mush. Of all the larger-leafed greens, I find chard's stems the most palatable. And because the stems are so colorful, they add visual interest to a dish. Their flavor and texture is somewhat like a softer, milder version of celery.

It isn't unheard of to eat raw chard, but the slightly bitter/salty flavor and chewy texture of the leaves don't particularly appeal to me, either massaged into a salad or whirred into a green smoothie. But if there's something about chard that speaks to you in its raw form, by all means, enjoy experimenting with it.

Although chard stands out as the star ingredient in simple preparations, it more than holds its own with bold-flavored grain, bean, and potato dishes, as well as in soups and stews.

Chard in Basic Preparations
Simple Garlicky Greens, page 40 ✑ Greens with Shallots & Olives, page 46 ✑ Chard with Raisins & Pecans, page 47 Chard with Brussels Sprouts & Red Peppers, page 50 Italian-Style Braised Chard with Tomatoes, page 57 Stir-Fried Chard with Napa Cabbage, page 74

Chard with Beans, Grains, Pasta & Other Vegetables
Quinoa with Chard & Chickpeas, page 82 ✑ Southwestern-Style Greens with Pinto Beans, page 105 ✑ Curried Sweet Potatoes with Chard & Chickpeas, page 106 ✑ Tostadas with Chili-Spiced Greens & Potatoes, page 110 ✑ White Bean & Greens Burgers, page 114 ✑ Pasta with Greens, Chickpeas & Olives, page 118 ✑ Italian Vegetable Ragout with Chard, page 126

COLLARD GREENS

Best known for their vaunted place in Southern cooking, collard greens were the biggest surprise for me as I developed recipes for this book. Although I wasn't completely unfamiliar with them, I had most often seen recipes for collards that called for boiling the leaves for 20 minutes or more or braising them for an equally long time, and each time I tried these techniques, I found the semi-mushy, olive-drab results less than exciting. But quick-braised or, better yet, stir-fried in narrow ribbons, this green is a standout, and its mild, sweet flavor is up there with the best of the leafy veggies. Maybe this shouldn't be such a surprise: Collard greens belong to the family of cruciferous vegetables that includes cabbage and broccoli, none of which are very appealing when overcooked. An easy way to cook collard greens while retaining their wonderful color and sweetness is to roll up the leaves, slice them very thinly, and stir-fry the ribbons until they're just tender-crisp.

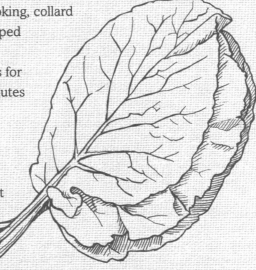

Because of their mild flavor, collard greens are amazingly good in stews and dishes that feature grains and beans, but they are just as delicious used in green juices and smoothies.

Collard Greens in Basic Preparations

Collard Greens with Beans, Grains, Pasta & Other Vegetables

Collard Greens in Juices & Smoothies

DANDELION GREENS

The leaves of this garden "weed" also come in a cultivated variety. Depending on size and age, the flavor of dandelion greens ranges from slightly sharp to downright bitter. Small, young leaves have the best flavor and texture and can be eaten raw; blanching larger leaves removes some of the bitterness (pages 13 and 38). Dandelion greens are usually sold in modest bunches. Because of that and their assertive flavor, they're not as versatile as other leafy greens. In this book, you'll find recipes for dandelion greens mainly in chapter 3, in salads, where they're combined with milder greens.

Dandelion Greens in Basic Preparations

Dandelion Greens in Salads

ESCAROLE

Escarole looks like a slightly denser, greener version of romaine lettuce, and is a much-loved vegetable in Italian cuisine. A member of the chicory family and a relative of curly endive and radicchio, escarole benefits from brief cooking to temper its mildly bitter bite.

If you enjoy a green that's slightly chewy and a bit bitter in your salads, you can shred escarole thinly and add a small quantity to a mix of milder salad greens. If you prefer escarole in cooked dishes, as I do, it wilts down quickly in sautés and becomes downright comforting in soups.

Escarole in Basic Preparations
Simple Garlicky Greens, page 40 ⊷ Chard with Brussels Sprouts & Red Peppers (variation), page 50 ⊷ Sautéed Escarole & Radicchio, page 51 ⊷ Citrus-Braised Escarole or Mustard Greens with Apples & Nuts, page 61

Escarole with Beans, Grains, Pasta & Other Vegetables
Ragout of Broccoli Rabe with White Beans & Porcini Mushrooms (variation), page 112 Pasta with Two Beans & Escarole, page 116 ⊷ Italian Vegetable Ragout with Chard (variation), page 126

Escarole in Soups & Stews
Hearty Italian-Flavored Chard & Vegetable Soup (variation), page 176 ⊷ Italian-Style Potato & Escarole Soup, page 178

KALE

Kale has become commonplace—it's the green that today seems to inspire the most overall devotion. I can't count how many times I've seen young people wearing sweatshirts and T-shirts reading "Kale University." And there's a bumper sticker that simply states, "I ❤ kale." Because it is as versatile as spinach, kale is one of the few greens in this book that makes multiple appearances in every chapter. There simply aren't many greens that work quite so well in a warming stew as they do in a refreshing beverage.

Like its cousin collard greens, kale is a cruciferous vegetable, a member of the family of veggies that broccoli and cauliflower belong to as well. Kale comes in several varieties. The three most commonly available are the ordinary curly-leafed type, lacinato (also called dinosaur kale), and Russian kale. Lacinato kale has long, narrow leaves that are a handsome, sometimes blue-green or forest green color. Russian Kale is also curly, with red-tipped leaves and a slightly less sweet flavor than its more common monochromatic green counterpart.

Although lacinato and Russian kale both look quite appealing, the mild, slightly sweet flavor of the more commonplace curly variety adapts best, in my opinion, to all manner of preparations. So while I gladly use lacinato and Russian kale in bold, cooked dishes like stews, the more common curly kale works best for me every time in raw salads, as well as in smoothies and juices.

Kale in Basic Preparations
Simple Garlicky Greens, page 40 ❧ Greens with Shallots & Olives, page 46 ❧ Braised Hardy Greens with Mixed Mushrooms, page 58 Stir-Fried Sesame Kale & Red Cabbage, page 70

Kale with Beans, Grains, Pasta & Other Vegetables
Quinoa with Chard and Chickpeas (variation), page 82
Quinoa with Kale, Sweet Potatoes & Pecans, page 85
Lemony Wild Rice with Greens, Pine Nuts & Raisins, page 91 ❧ Black Rice with Black-Eyed Peas & Greens, page 92 ❧ Curried Sweet Potatoes with Chard & Chickpeas (variation), page 106 ❧ Tostadas with Chili-Spiced Greens & Potatoes, page 111
Ragout of Broccoli Rabe with White Beans &

Curly Kale

Lacinato Kale

Kale in Salads

Kale in Soups & Stews

Kale in Juices & Smoothies

MIZUNA

Mizuna, which resembles young arugula in flavor and appearance, is a member of the mustard family that originated in Japan. Its small, deep green, sawtooth leaves add a mildly sweet and spicy flavor to mixed salads, as well as a pleasant visual appeal. Mizuna is delicious steamed, stir-fried, or wilted in soups.

Even if you're unfamiliar with mizuna, you may have had it without realizing it, since it is often mixed in with other greens in commercially prepared bags of salad. These days, mizuna is increasingly available at farmers' markets and CSA (Community Supported Agriculture) farms. If the opportunity comes your way, it's well worth trying this light, leafy green.

MUSTARD GREENS

I didn't have much to do with mustard greens before starting to research this book. Since I'm not a huge fan of spiciness, I was put off just by the name, and the sheer size of mustard green bunches can seem daunting to the uninitiated. But I'm happy to say I've become a convert. The flavor of mustard greens has been described as pungent or peppery, though I'd characterize it as sharp, like horseradish. Like many greens that have a certain bite to them, mustard greens mellow quite a bit when they're lightly cooked.

RADISH GREENS

Like turnips and beets, radish greens come in modest quantities. The greens on
a decent-size bunch of radishes, which constitute little more than a handful—are
particularly perishable and often have to be winnowed of at least a few leaves that
are past their prime. If you have these easy-to-grow veggies fresh at hand from your
garden, though, you'll be able to make more use of them.

Why bother with radish greens? Well, they are delightfully tender and mildly
spicy, and they're a great treat, either sautéed with radishes or tossed together into
green salads.

SPINACH

Although spinach is considered a cool-weather garden green, it's available year-round, and its mild flavor makes it one of the most popular and versatile of all the leafy greens—along with kale, it makes the most appearances in this book and is covered in every chapter. Whether completely blended into a refreshing juice or smoothie or placed at the heart of a salad, spinach is a nutritious superstar. It's widely known and a staple in many cuisines around the world.

Spinach comes in a surprising array of varieties, with leaf types ranging from flat to semi-savoyed (a.k.a. "crinkled") or heavily savoyed, with a range of poetic names like Melody, Marathon, Bloomsdale, and Five-star. Leaf sizes vary from baby spinach to the large, almost chard-like Malabar or summer spinach. With the exception of the latter variety—which, like chard, is enhanced with light cooking, most other kinds of spinach are tender and equally good used raw or very lightly cooked. "Lightly" is the operative word here. With the exception of summer spinach, other varieties are at their best with the briefest of wilting.

Spinach in Basic Preparations

Simple Garlicky Greens, page 40 ❧ Mediterranean Greens with Pine Nuts & Raisins, page 44 ❧ Spring Greens Sauté with Carrots, Mint & Chives, page 45 ❧ Indian-Style Mustard Greens with Spinach, page 62 ❧ Spring Greens Stir-Fry, page 72

Spinach with Beans, Grains, Pasta & Other Vegetables

Quinoa with Baby Bok Choy & Asparagus, page 86 ❧ Polenta or Grits with Spinach & Caramelized Onions, page 87 ❧ Bok Choy Fried Rice (variation), page 88 ❧ Dilled Spinach Rice, page 90 ❧ Persian Spinach with Black-Eyed Peas & Herbs, page 95 ❧ Southwestern-Style Greens with Pinto Beans, page 105 ❧ Curried Sweet Potatoes with Chard & Chickpeas (variation), page 106 ❧ Tostadas with Chili-Spiced Greens & Potatoes, page 110 ❧ White Bean & Greens Burgers, page 114 ❧ Pasta with Asparagus, Arugula & Sun-Dried Tomatoes (variation), page 117 ❧ Pasta with Greens, Chickpeas & Olives, page 118 ❧ Pad See Ew (variation), page 122 ❧ Greens with Polenta Wedges, page 128 ❧ Roasted Eggplant Curry with Greens & Tomatoes, page 140

Spinach in Salads

Spinach in Soups & Stews

Spinach in Juices & Smoothies

TATSOI

In their raw form, these small, dark, spoon-shaped, and mild-flavored leaves are perfect in salads and wilt quickly into stir-fries—much like spinach.

Tatsoi in Basic Preparations

Tatsoi with Beans, Grains, Pasta & Other Vegetables

Tatsoi in Salads

Tatsoi in Soups & Stews

TURNIP GREENS

When you purchase turnip greens at the store you come away with a modest amount of greens, just as you do with beets. Turnip greens taste similar to the turnip itself but have more of a bite. The larger the leaves, the more pungent and bitter they become. Among dark leafy greens, turnip greens stack up extremely well in the nutrition department and have a particularly good calcium profile. Along with mustard greens, they are a versatile, delicious component of traditional Southern cooking and soul food.

Even though it may not be easy to get your hands on a really big bunch of turnip greens, it's worth seeking them out and enjoying their distinctive flavor, particularly in combination with milder greens.

Turnip Greens in Basic Preparations
Simple Garlicky Greens, page 40 ⮞ Sautéed Mustard Greens & Turnip Greens, page 52 ⮞ Turnips or Radishes & Their Greens, page 56

Turnip Greens with Beans, Grains, Pasta & Other Vegetables
Black Rice with Black-Eyed Peas & Greens, page 92
Tostadas with Chili-Spiced Greens & Potatoes, page 112
Smoky Potatoes with Turnip Greens (variation), page 139

Turnip Greens in Salads
Raw Turnips or Radishes & Their Greens, page 165

WATERCRESS

To use the word "peppery" to describe the flavor of this tiny green is to invoke a culinary cliché, but there's really no other word for it. A member of the mustard family, watercress has a pleasantly peppery taste that comes from mustard oils that are released when the leaves are chewed. It's a mildly hot and flavorful bite that makes this tender green that's rich in vitamin C easy to love. It used to be that the appearance of watercress at the market was a harbinger of spring, just like asparagus, but now it's available year-round. All the greens in this book are nutritional powerhouses, but watercress is believed to have healing and tonic properties above and beyond its splendid concentration of vitamins and minerals.

Watercress—small, round, mid-tone green leaves atop long, slender stems—is usually sold in bouquet-like bundles. The stems are edible, and you can use as much or as little of them as you choose. Watercress is delicious eaten raw in salads and is interchangeable with lettuce in sandwiches, delivering a spicy crunch. You can also add watercress to soups, at the last minute, for extra flavor and a mild heat, or wilt it into in stir-fries.

Watercress in Basic Preparations
Spring Greens Sauté with Carrots, Mint & Chives, page 45

Watercress with Greens with Beans, Grains, Pasta & Other Vegetables
Quinoa with Baby Bok Choy & Asparagus, page 86

Watercress in Salads
Spring Greens & Berries Salad, page 154 ᘓ Orange & Cucumber Salad with Spring Greens, page 155 ᘓ Sumptuous Spring Greens Salad, page 156 ᘓ Grated Carrot Salad with Watercress & Parsley, page 157 ᘓ Pinto Bean Salad with Watercress & Dill, page 158 Spinach, Watercress & Bok Choy Salad, page 159 ᘓ Dilled Watercress & Silken Tofu Dip, page 172

Watercress in Soups & Stews
Puree of Green Peas & Spring Greens, page 188
Red Lentil Dal with Red Beans & Greens, page 190
Leek & Potato Soup with Watercress, page 191
Quick Quinoa & Spring Greens Soup, page 193

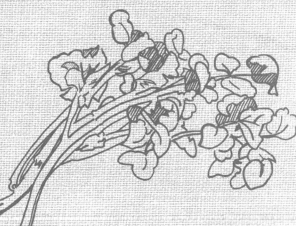

CHAPTER I

BASIC PREPARATIONS FOR LEAFY GREENS

The original title of this chapter was "Side Dishes," but I quickly realized how woefully inadequate it was to describe these recipes. Though it's unlikely you'll make any of them as the main course (no matter what your dietary persuasion), you'll find that greens, no matter how simply prepared, never sit quietly by as a mere "side." This chapter demonstrates some of the basic techniques and recipes for preparing a wide variety of greens so they can really shine, from familiar garlicky sautés, to braises, stir-fries, and more. Once you've mastered these techniques, feel free to explore the interchangeability of greens in basic preparations by substituting whatever you have on hand. As a special bonus, on page 78 of this chapter, you'll find a recipe for Oven-Baked Kale Chips —the snack no kale aficionado can get enough of.

SIMPLE SAUTÉS

Simple Garlicky Greens, 40

Mediterranean Greens with Pine Nuts & Raisins, 44

Spring Greens Sauté with Carrots, Mint & Chives, 45

Greens with Shallots & Olives, 46

Chard with Raisins & Pecans, 47

Chard with Brussels Sprouts & Red Peppers, 50

Sautéed Escarole & Radicchio, 51

Sautéed Mustard Greens & Turnip Greens, 52

Sweet & Citrusy Beets with Their Greens, 54

BRAISED GREENS

Italian-Style Braised Chard with Tomatoes, 57

Braised Hardy Greens with Mixed Mushrooms, 58

Wine & Mustard–Braised Asian Greens, 60

Citrus-Braised Escarole or Mustard Greens with Apples & Nuts, 61

Indian-Style Mustard Greens with Spinach, 62

SAUCES FOR SIMPLY COOKED GREENS

"Mustard Greens" Sauce, 64

Tahini-Lemon Sauce, 64

Spicy Peanut or Cashew Sauce, 65

Avocado-Tahini Dressing, 66

CLASSIC STIR-FRIES

Basic Stir-Fried Asian Greens, 68

Stir-Fried Bok Choy & Snow Peas with Shiitake Mushrooms, 69

Stir-Fried Sesame Kale & Red Cabbage, 70

Spring Greens Stir-Fry, 72

Stir-Fried Chard with Napa Cabbage, 74

Stir-Fried Collard Greens with Variations, 76

BASIC TECHNIQUES FOR PREPARING GREENS

When it comes to preparing greens simply and quickly, a few complementary ingredients and flavorings are particularly delicious. Garlic, of course, is at the top of the list; onions, leeks, and shallots are good companions as well. I can't quite explain it, but I find shallots particularly good with greens. Give these mild, sweet, oniony bulbs a try if they're not already a staple in your kitchen.

Lemon juice and apple cider vinegar are traditional seasonings for greens. Use them with a light hand and they'll brighten the mild flavors of cooked greens. If you like your greens spicy, a fresh hot chili pepper or two, seeded or minced, will do the trick. Or if you like spice but want a shortcut, sprinkle on a few dried hot red pepper flakes.

For an Asian spin, give soy sauce, tamari, or miso a try. These sauces, made from fermented soybeans, impart a salty flavor, with some subtle differences. If you use soy sauce, try a natural, long-fermented brand. This is the kind most often available in natural foods stores rather than supermarkets. Tamari, the Japanese version of soy sauce, is thicker, with a more complex, less overwhelmingly salty flavor. Both are available in reduced-sodium, gluten-free versions. Bragg Liquid Aminos is also a non–genetically modified soy-based, gluten-free seasoning that's enriched with sixteen amino acids. Popular with a lot of natural foods devotees, the stuff is delicious. However, a small controversy has been brewing lately about some naturally occurring MSG in Liquid Aminos, which will probably turn out to be a tempest in a teapot (or a bottle, as the case may be), so for now I'll stay out of the fray. Any of these salty liquids can quickly overpower the flavor of lightly cooked greens if they're not used sparingly, so use a gentle hand with them.

Ginger and shiitake mushrooms are two other ingredients that enhance simple preparations of Asian-flavored greens.

SIMPLY STEAMING OR WILTING GREENS

For tender greens like spinach, arugula, beet greens, smaller chard leaves, young dandelion greens, mustard greens, mizuna, tatsoi, and other Asian greens, steaming and wilting are the simplest methods of all.

Steaming requires a little water at the bottom of the pan. I like to use water no more than ¼ inch in depth—just enough to keep the bottom of the pan and the greens moist, but not so much as to create a pool of water in which to lose valuable vitamins and minerals.

Wilting uses just the water that clings to the leaves. Once your greens are washed and stemmed and while the leaves still retain a sheen of water, heat a small soup pot or a steep-sided stir-fry pan. Add the greens a batch at a time. Cover and let the greens cook down until they're just wilted and bright green. This takes only 1 to 3 minutes, depending on the amount and variety of the greens. Remove them from the heat and serve the greens plain with salt and pepper, or add them to other preparations. You can swirl wilted greens into soups, stews, or grain dishes at the last minute before serving or blend them into dips or pestos.

To create delicious side dishes, try adding these simple embellishments to your steamed or wilted greens:

- Halved cherry tomatoes
- White beans or chickpeas
- Sweet chili sauce
- Dried hot red pepper flakes
- Sesame seeds
- A drizzle of sesame oil with soy sauce or tamari

SAUTÉING GREENS

Sautéing, like steaming or wilting, is another excellent method of preparing tender greens like spinach, arugula, beet greens, smaller chard leaves, young dandelion greens, mustard greens, mizuna, tatsoi, and other Asian greens. Once greens are washed, stemmed (and, if need be, chopped), let them dry a bit. A little water clinging to the leaves is fine, but they shouldn't be wet.

Heat some olive oil in a large skillet. If you'd like, start by sautéing some garlic and/ or shallots for a minute or two over low heat. Raise the heat to medium-high and add the greens, in batches, to a pan that can comfortably hold all of them. Gently stirring, sauté the greens until all of them are in the pan. Sprinkle in a little salt, if you like; it will tenderize the leaves and help them retain their green color. A drizzle of apple cider vinegar, lemon juice, soy sauce, or tamari are other good options for flavoring your greens.

Sauté the greens until they're tender, erring on the side of less cooking time rather than more, since greens will continue to wilt after they've been removed from the heat. Sautéing is an ideal way to prepare greens, especially if you intend to serve them right away.

BLANCHING GREENS

While blanching is the preferred method for freezing greens, most recipes don't require it. One notable exception in this book is the recipe for Collard-Wrapped Yellow Rice and Black Bean Enchiladas (page 180), which does require blanching to make the leaves more palatable. But if you'd like to use this basic technique to wilt down greens like collards, kales, and large sturdy chards rather than steaming or sautéing them (a method that doesn't work nearly as well with hardier greens) it couldn't be simpler.

Cut leaves away from the stems and wash them well. Bring a large pot of water to a boil, then plunge the leaves into it and cook them for a minute or two, just until they turn bright green. Drain the leaves, then chop them as desired. Add the blanched greens to soups, stews, and sautés toward the end of the cooking time.

Blanching is also the preferred way to remove bitterness from large, tough dandelion greens. Simply wash the greens well, trim away any tough stems, and proceed as described above, immersing the leaves into boiling water for about a minute. Drain the greens, run them under cool water, and then chop. The blanched dandelion greens can then be used in Simple Garlicky Greens (page 40) and Spring Greens Stir-Fry (page 72).

BRAISING GREENS

Braising is a great technique for hardier greens like collards, kale, and broccoli rabe, and also works nicely for greens that don't wilt on contact, like chard and mustard greens. A braise starts out just like a sauté: First, heat olive oil in a large skillet, and if you like, sauté some garlic and/or shallots for a minute or two over low heat. Raise the heat to medium-high and add the greens in batches. Sauté and stir the leaves until all of them are in the pan. Quickly sprinkle in a little salt to help tenderize the greens and allow them to retain their bright green color.

Add a bit of liquid; this can be water, vegetable stock, or wine—not a huge amount, just enough to keep the pan moist. About ½ inch of liquid in the bottom of the pan is about right, which adds up to ¼ to ½ cup of liquid, depending on the amount of greens you're cooking. Cook and stir the greens until they're just tender. Cover them briefly to hasten the process. You can pour out the excess liquid, or add a little dissolved flour or cornstarch to thicken the liquid into a sauce.

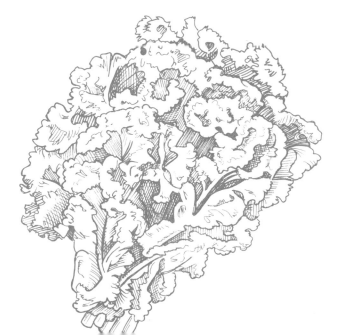

SIMPLE SAUTÉS

Simple Garlicky Greens (with lots of variations)

4 to 6 servings

If there could be only one recipe in the world for leafy greens, I'd vote for this one. Besides being my favorite, it also defies the notion that certain greens—notably collards—have to be cooked in a big pot of boiling water. This quick-cooking method is a basic sauté for tender greens and a braise for hardier leaves. The main idea is to cook the greens as little as possible, so they retain their color, flavor, and texture. When you want to cook a bigger batch of greens, or if you just want a change of pace, try combining a more intense green with a milder one, such as chard with arugula or mustard greens with spinach (see a braise of this combination, Indian-Style Mustard Greens with Spinach, on page 62). Be sure to add greens that cook quickly into the cooking process after you've begun with the slower-cooking greens. You can also combine greens with cabbage in this simple preparation. Kale and chard are particularly good sautéed with napa cabbage (see Stir-Fried Chard with Napa Cabbage, on page 74).

> 1 **good-size bunch (12 ounces to 1¼ pounds) greens of your choice —any variety of spinach, kale, collards, chard, turnip greens, mustard greens, escarole, broccoli rabe, or blanched dandelion greens (page 38)**
>
> 1 **to 2 tablespoons extra-virgin olive oil**
>
> 3 **to 4 cloves garlic, crushed**
>
> **Juice of ½ to 1 lemon, or apple cider vinegar, to taste**
>
> **Salt and freshly ground pepper to taste**

Cut leaves away from stems if using kale, collards, chard, or turnip greens. If you'd like to use the stems from curly kale or chard in this preparation, slice them thinly (stems from lacinato kale and collards tend to be tough and not very tasty). If using curly kale, cut the leaves into bite-size pieces. If using greens with flatter leaves, like lacinato kale, collards, or flatter varieties of chard, stack a few leaves at a time, roll snugly from one of the narrow ends, then slice thinly. Chop in a few places to shorten the ribbons.

If using mustard greens or escarole, just slice the leaves, and include the midribs, which are tender.

For broccoli rabe, trim a half-inch or so off the base of the stems, slice them into ½- to 1-inch sections, and use the stems, florets, and leaves.

If using regular spinach, remove most long stems. Baby spinach can be left whole.

Heat the oil in a large steep-sided skillet or stir-fry pan. Add the garlic and sauté over low heat for 2 to 3 minutes, until golden.

Add the greens and cook over medium heat, stirring frequently until just tender. Add small amounts of water, wine, or vegetable broth, if needed—just enough to keep the bottom of the pan moist. Spinach takes the least amount of time; basically you just want to wilt it, which takes only a minute or so. To cook until just tender but still nice and green, chard and kale take about 5 to 7 minutes, and broccoli rabe and collards take about 5 to 8 minutes or slightly longer. The variables are how high your heat is and how thinly you've cut your greens.

Add the lemon juice or vinegar (for darker greens use balsamic vinegar in place of apple cider vinegar or lemon juice). Season with salt and pepper, and serve.

Sweet Additions
Once the greens are cooked, stir in ¼ to ½ cup raisins, dried cranberries, currants, or sliced dried apricots or figs. Figs are especially good with chard. Caramelized onions and shallots add an earthy sweetness, as well.

Nutty Additions
Sprinkle ¼ to ½ cup toasted nuts over the top of the greens in the pan prior to serving. Try any of the following:

- ✒ Pine nuts
- ✒ Almonds (slivered or sliced)
- ✒ Pecans (chopped)
- ✒ Walnuts (chopped)

Savory Additions

Once the greens are cooked, stir in any of these:
- ✒ ½ cup or so sliced brine-cured olives (kalamatas are particularly good)
- ✒ ½ cup or so of sliced sun-dried tomatoes (oil-cured or not, as you prefer)
- ✒ 2 to 3 tablespoons capers

Spicy Additions

Stir any of the following into cooked greens, to your taste:
- ✒ Dried hot red pepper flakes to taste
- ✒ Fresh seeded and minced hot chili pepper
- ✒ Chili oil, Thai red chili paste, or any hot sauce or condiment to taste

A Creamy Variation

Puree a 12.3-ounce box of silken tofu in the container of a food processor. Add the cooked greens and pulse and on and off until they're finely chopped (don't puree) and completely integrated with the tofu. This makes a tasty side dish that you can serve with just about anything.

Basic Pureed Greens

If you're chopping these Simple Garlicky Greens in the food processor, just keep the machine going until the greens are pureed. You can use this puree over grains or mashed potatoes, or use a generous dollop to garnish pureed soups, especially butternut squash, pumpkin, sweet potato, or carrot. The contrasting colors are a treat to the eye as well as the palate.

GREEN UP YOUR CARBS

If you're serving potatoes, rice, or other grains as side dishes, a dose of greens ramps up the flavor and nutrition in mild-flavored starches.

An easy way to do this is to follow the recipe for Simple Garlicky Greens (page 40). Then either transfer the cooked greens to a food processor and pulse on and off until the greens are finely chopped, or transfer them to a cutting board and chop the greens finely by hand. Quantity doesn't matter very much—8 to 12 ounces of an average bunch of greens works well when it's incorporated into a carbohydrate-rich dish that serves 4 to 6. For example, instead of serving plain brown rice on its own, as a side dish, you can ramp up the flavor and nutrition of the rice by several notches if you stir into it some finely chopped, lightly cooked greens.

For greening up carbs I recommend milder greens such as spinach (any variety), kale (any variety, but in my opinion curly kale works best), collard greens, and chard. Slightly bitter or sharp greens like mustard greens, escarole, or even arugula can overpower mild grains.

Try stirring finely chopped cooked greens into:
- Brown rice, or any of the more exotic types such as basmati, forbidden black rice, jasmine, etc.
- Wild rice
- Mashed or sautéed white, golden, or sweet potatoes
- Risotto
- Quinoa, millet, barley, and any other cooked healthy whole grains

Mediterranean Greens with Pine Nuts & Raisins

4 to 6 servings

Here's a traditional Italian recipe for greens that's both elegant and easy. The sweetness of raisins provides a nice contrast to the greens, especially the broccoli rabe, and tempers its slight bitterness.

>   1   tablespoon extra-virgin olive oil
>   2   to 3 cloves garlic, minced
>   3   to 4 shallots, thinly sliced, optional
>   2   to 3 tablespoons pine nuts
> 10   to 12 ounces spinach (any variety), chard, or broccoli rabe
>   1   tablespoon lemon juice
>   ¼   to ½ cup raisins, to taste
>   Salt and freshly ground pepper to taste

Heat the oil in a large skillet or steep-sided stir-fry pan. Add the garlic and the shallots (if you're using them), and sauté over low heat for 1 minute, stirring frequently. Add the pine nuts and continue to sauté, stirring often, until they and the garlic are golden, about 3 minutes longer.

If you're using spinach, stem, and chop the leaves (baby spinach leaves can be used whole). If you're using chard, cut the leaves away from the stems and chop them into bite-size pieces. If you'd like to use the stems, trim an inch off the bottoms, then slice them thinly. For broccoli rabe, trim a half-inch or so off the base of the stems, slice them into ½- to 1-inch sections, and then use the stems, florets, and leaves.

Add the greens, cover, and set the heat to medium. For spinach, uncover and stir, then cover and cook just a minute or so longer, until the leaves are just wilted and still bright green. For chard and broccoli rabe, add tiny amounts of water to the pan, just enough to keep it moist; cook for 3 to 5 minutes longer for the chard, and 5 to 7 minutes longer for the broccoli rabe. The greens should be just tender, and the exact time will depend on the heat and the way they are cut.

Once the greens are cooked to your liking, remove them from the heat. Stir in the lemon juice and raisins, then season with salt and pepper and serve at once.

Spring Greens Sauté with Carrots, Mint & Chives

4 servings

Here's a fresh-tasting sauté that's ready in minutes.

- 2 **tablespoons extra-virgin olive oil**
- 2 **to 3 cloves garlic, minced**
- 12 **or so baby carrots, quartered lengthwise**
- 6 **to 8 ounces baby spinach, large stems removed**
- 2 **to 4 ounces baby arugula leaves, large stems removed**
- **Tender dandelion greens, radish greens, and/or watercress, as desired**
- 1 **tablespoon lemon juice, or to taste**
- 8 **to 12 fresh mint leaves (or more, to taste), sliced**
- **Minced fresh chives to taste**
- **Salt and freshly ground pepper to taste**

Heat the oil in a large skillet or steep-sided stir-fry pan. Add the garlic and carrots and sauté over low heat for 1 to 2 minutes, stirring frequently.

Add the greens, as many as the pan will comfortably accommodate, stirring continuously and adding batches until all the greens are in the pan. Cook only until the greens are wilted down and bright green. This entire process should take no more than 2 to 3 minutes.

Stir in the lemon juice, mint, and chives. Season with salt and pepper and serve at once.

Greens with Shallots & Olives

4 to 6 servings

Marie Panesko, a longtime reader of mine, contributed the idea for this simple, tasty side dish. Although her original preparation is made with chard, it's good with kale or collard greens as well. Serve these delicious greens on their own or atop pasta, grains, or soft polenta.

- **10 to 12 ounces hardy greens (such as chard, lacinato kale, or collard greens)**
- **1 tablespoon extra-virgin olive oil**
- **3 to 4 shallots, or more, to taste, thinly sliced**
- **2 cloves garlic, minced, optional**
- **¼ cup white wine or water**
- **½ cup cured pitted black olives (such as Kalamata), sliced**
- **Dried hot red pepper flakes to taste**
- **Salt and freshly ground pepper to taste**

Cut the leaves away from the stems. Unless you're using chard, discard the stems. If using chard, slice the stems thinly. Stack a few leaves at a time; roll them up snugly from one of the narrow ends, then cut the roll into ½-inch ribbons. Chop the ribbons in a few places to shorten them; repeat with all the leaves.

Heat the oil in a medium skillet. Add the shallots and optional garlic, and sauté over low heat until golden.

Add the wine or water and as many of the greens as will fit comfortably in the pan. Cover the greens and allow them to wilt down briefly; continue to add the chard until all of it is in the pan. Cook the greens over medium heat, stirring them frequently, for about 5 to 7 minutes, or until the greens are tender but still nice and bright.

Stir in the olives, then add just enough red pepper flakes to give the greens a subtle heat. Season with salt and pepper (you won't need much salt, if any). Serve at once.

Chard with Raisins & Pecans

4 servings

This richly flavored chard dish was contributed by Shen J. C. Robinson, who, like the contributor of the previous recipe, is a longtime reader of mine. It's delicious served over soft polenta or grains, or just on its own.

10 to 12 ounces chard, any variety

1 tablespoon extra-virgin olive oil

3 to 4 cloves garlic, minced

¼ cup marsala or other dry red wine

⅓ cup raisins

1 tablespoon capers, optional

Salt and freshly ground pepper to taste

⅓ to ½ cup finely chopped pecans

Cut the leaves away from the stems. Trim about an inch from the bottom of the stems, then slice thinly, or if you prefer, discard them (this dish is particularly beautiful and tasty, though, with thinly sliced rainbow chard stems). Stack a few leaves at a time and cut them into ½-inch ribbons. Chop the ribbons in a few places to shorten them; repeat this process with all the leaves.

Heat the oil in a medium skillet. Add the garlic and sauté over low heat until golden. Add the marsala wine and as much chard as will fit comfortably in the pan. Cover and allow the greens to wilt down briefly; continue to add the chard until all of it is in the pan. Cook, covered, until the leaves are tender, about 5 minutes.

Stir in the raisins and the capers, if you're using them, then season with salt and pepper. Scatter the pecans over the top and serve at once.

Variations

This recipe works well with chopped or sliced kale (any variety), collard greens (cut into narrow ribbons), and spinach (any variety).

GREENS ON THE GRILL

Your grilling unit offers yet another way to prepare leafy greens. Some greens lend themselves to grilling better than others. Not surprisingly, sturdy greens with lots of surface, like broccoli rabe and baby bok choy, work well, while there's no reason on earth to cook delicate baby arugula or watercress over the flames.

Grilling greens can involve some enjoyable experimentation on your part, and the outcome will vary depending on the kind of unit you use. An indoor/outdoor electric grill is the easiest to control when you're cooking leafy greens. In fact, you can place them right on the grill surface and adjust the heat setting as needed. With other grills, you'll want to use a grill basket so that the greens don't fall through.

No matter what kind of grill you use—electric, charcoal, or gas—the idea is to cook the greens quickly to bring out deep flavor without totally charring the leaves. Once they've acquired those attractive grill marks, they're ready to eat. Here are the greens, I've found, that cook best on the grill:

BROCCOLI RABE: Separate the bunch into sections that include one or two of the florets. Before grilling, rub them lightly with olive oil or any healthy vegetable oil of your choice. Grill for 5 to 8 minutes total, depending on the heat level of your grill, using tongs to turn the sections every couple of minutes.

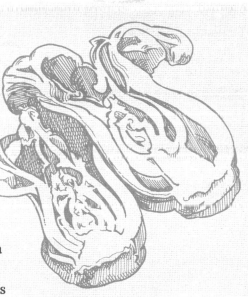

BABY BOK CHOY: Cut the choy in half, as described in the sidebar for Seared Baby Bok Choy (page 75), and rub it lightly with vegetable oil. You can also use Sesame-Ginger Salad Dressing (page 168) as a marinade. Grill the bok choy for 3 to 4 minutes per side, or until grill marks appear, using tongs to turn it over.

ESCAROLE: Cut a head of escarole into quarters, right through the stem, so that the leaves remain connected. It's easiest to give the leaves a light coating with an olive oil cooking spray; otherwise, drizzle them with olive oil and rub it into the leaves as best you can. Grill them for 3 to 4 minutes per side, or until grill marks appear on the leaves. Use tongs to turn them over.

One more idea—make kale chips on the grill. Cut washed and dried curly kale leaves into large bite-size pieces. Rub olive oil into the leaves until they're evenly coated. Place them in a grill basket (even if you're using the electric grill, since this makes it easier to stir them) and cook the leaves until they are crisp and starting to turn brown. Use a small metal spatula to stir them frequently. Season the kale as you would oven-baked kale chips (see suggestions on page 78).

Chard with Brussels Sprouts & Red Peppers

4 to 6 servings

Brussels sprouts look pretty when they are halved and mingled with leafy greens—
and they taste wonderful together, too.

10 to 12 ounces brussels sprouts, stemmed and halved

10 to 12 ounces chard, any variety

2 tablespoons extra-virgin olive oil

2 cloves garlic, minced

1 medium red bell pepper, finely diced

1 tablespoon lemon juice (or more, to taste)

Salt and freshly ground pepper to taste

¼ cup chopped toasted walnuts
or 2 to 3 tablespoons toasted pine nuts, optional

In a large skillet, combine the brussels sprouts with about $1/2$ cup water. Cover and cook the sprouts for about 5 to 7 minutes, until they are tender-crisp. Drain the sprouts, put them in a bowl, and set them aside.

Meanwhile, cut the leaves from the chard stems. If you are using the stems, trim about 1 inch from the bottoms, then thinly slice them. Discard the stems if you are not using them. Stack several leaves and slice them into ribbons, about ½ inch wide.

Heat the oil in the skillet. Add the garlic, bell pepper, and chard (along with stems if you're using them). Sauté the chard over medium heat for 4 to 5 minutes until it is tender to your liking.

Place the brussels sprouts back in the skillet, season them with the lemon juice, salt, and pepper, and stir. Scatter the nuts over the top, if you're using them, and serve at once, directly from the skillet.

Variation
Try this dish with mustard greens or escarole if you enjoy a sharper flavor.

Sautéed Escarole & Radicchio

4 to 6 servings

Raisins and breadcrumbs mellow the flavor of this mildly bitter green-and-red duo. Both of these leafy veggies are well loved in Italian cuisine.

2 average-size slices whole-grain bread

½ medium head escarole or mustard greens

1 small head radicchio

2 tablespoons extra-virgin olive oil

2 to 3 cloves garlic, minced

⅓ cup raisins

½ cup minced fresh parsley

¼ cup sliced fresh basil leaves, optional

Salt and freshly ground pepper to taste

Toast the bread until it's golden brown. Tear it into several pieces and place it in a food processor. Process the bread into coarse crumbs. Set them aside until needed.

Cut the greens and radicchio crosswise into long ribbons. Place them in a colander and rinse well.

Heat the oil in a large skillet. Add the garlic and sauté over low heat until golden. Add the greens and radicchio. Sauté them over medium-high heat, stirring frequently, for about 6 to 8 minutes, or until both are tender.

Stir in the raisins, parsley, and optional basil. Season with salt and pepper. Sprinkle the breadcrumbs over the top and serve at once straight from the pan.

Sautéed Mustard Greens & Turnip Greens

4 to 6 servings

In Southern cooking and soul food these two pungent greens are sometimes prepared together, usually with bacon or a ham hock. In lieu of these, I've added a bit of spice and some smoky flavorings to approximate the traditional seasoning. The leafy duo of mustard and turnip greens mellows quite a bit when cooked. This recipe makes a flavorful and supremely nutritious "mess of greens."

1   **tablespoon olive oil**
    or other healthy vegetable oil

1   **medium onion, quartered and thinly sliced**

3   **to 4 cloves garlic, minced**

1   **head mustard greens, stemmed, washed, and chopped**
    (about 10 to 12 ounces)

8   **ounces turnip greens (or whatever dark leafy green is available),**
    stemmed and chopped

2   **tablespoons apple cider vinegar**

2   **teaspoons natural granulated sugar**

½   **teaspoon mesquite-flavored seasoning,**
    or ½ teaspoon liquid smoke-flavored seasoning

    Salt and freshly ground pepper to taste

Heat the oil in a large, steep-sided skillet or stir-fry pan. Add the onion and sauté over medium heat until it's translucent; add the garlic and continue to sauté until both are lightly browned.

Add the mustard greens and turnip greens in batches until they're all in pan, stirring continuously. If needed, add small amounts of water—just enough to keep the pan moist, but not so much as to make this a braise.

Cover and cook the greens over medium heat until they've just lost their raw quality, about 3 minutes. Drizzle the vinegar and then sprinkle the sugar and seasoning over the greens.

Cook for a minute or two longer. Remove the greens from the heat when they are tender to your liking and still have a bright color. Serve them at once.

Variation

No turnip greens? Combine the mustard greens with another dark leafy green such as spinach or chard.

Sweet & Citrusy Beets with Their Greens

4 to 6 servings

One of the most basic ways to use beets is to serve them with their nourishing greens. Here's a simple preparation using both orange and lemon juice, flavors that nicely complement both the beets and the greens.

- **1 good-size bunch of beets with greens (4 large or 6 medium beets)**
- **2 teaspoons cornstarch or arrowroot**
- **Juice of ½ to 1 lemon, to taste**
- **½ cup orange juice, preferably fresh**
- **1 tablespoon agave nectar**
- **Salt and freshly ground pepper to taste**
- **2 tablespoons minced fresh dill, optional**

Remove the greens from the beets, leaving about ¼ inch of the stalk on the beets.

To prepare the beets, you can either cook or microwave them. To cook them, place the beets in a saucepan that will comfortably hold them, and cover with water. Bring the water to a boil, then lower the heat and simmer over medium-low heat for 20 to 30 minutes, or until the beets are just tender. Alternatively, place the beets in a covered microwave-safe container with a small amount of water at the bottom; microwave on high, allowing 2 minutes per beet. Add more time as needed until the beets can be pierced easily but aren't overdone.

Drain the beets and let them sit in a bowl of cold water while you prepare the greens. Wash the leaves and cut them away from the midribs. Chop them into bite-size pieces; then, with the water clinging to their leaves, place them in a steep-sided skillet or stir-fry pan. Cover the leaves and cook them down for about 3 minutes, until they're just wilted and bright green. Remove from the heat.

Trim the roots and tops from the beets and peel them. Slice them ¼ inch thick, or cut them into large dice, whichever appeals to you more.

In a small bowl, combine the cornstarch with just enough water to dissolve it. Add the lemon and orange juices and the agave nectar and whisk together.

Add the diced beets to the pan and stir together with the greens. Return the pan to medium heat. Pour in the citrus mixture and cook, stirring continuously, until a sauce thickens. Season with salt and pepper; sprinkle in the dill, if you're using it, and serve at once.

PREPARING TURNIPS OR RADISHES
& THEIR GREENS

Even though turnips and radishes usually don't come with a huge bunch of greens, there are enough leaves on the plants to embellish the texture and flavor of the veggies when you cook them together. This basic preparation is perfect for those times when your turnips or radishes come with a nice bunch of greens attached to them. It doesn't require exact quantities. Just grab what you've brought in from your garden or the farmers' market—4 to 6 medium turnips and their greens, say, or a nice bunch of radishes, a dozen or more.

FOR TURNIPS: Trim away and discard the stems and thick midribs from the greens. Coarsely chop the greens or cut them into strips. Wash them very well, then coarsely chop and set them aside. If the turnips and greens look muddy, give them a bath in a bowl of water and swish them around to loosen dirt. Scoop them out and give them another rinse in a colander. Pare the turnips and cut them into ½-inch dice.

FOR RADISHES: Trim the long tails from the bottoms, then cut the stems off as close as possible to the radishes. Cut most of the stems away from the leaves. Discard leaves that are yellowed or wilted. Since radishes grow so close to the ground, the leaves are often pretty muddy. Definitely give them a bath or two in a bowl of water to loosen the dirt, and give them a final rinse in a colander. Chop the leaves coarsely. Cut larger radishes into quarters, smaller ones in half.

TO SAUTÉ: Heat enough olive oil to lightly coat a medium skillet. Sauté the turnips or radishes for 3 to 5 minutes, stirring them frequently, until they are golden on most sides and still tender-crisp.

Stir in the greens. Sauté them over medium heat for no more than 2 to 3 minutes, stirring continuously, until the leaves are wilted and bright green. If you like, drizzle in a teaspoon or two of apple cider vinegar, then season to taste with salt and pepper.

BRAISED GREENS

Italian-Style Braised Chard with Tomatoes

4 to 6 servings

Since chard is so beloved in Italy and other parts of the
Mediterranean, it's only fitting to combine it with tomatoes,
basil, and other flavorings typical of the region's cuisines.

10 **to 12 ounces chard, any variety**

2 **tablespoons extra-virgin olive oil**

½ **medium red onion, thinly sliced**

3 **to 4 cloves garlic, minced or sliced**

¼ **cup white wine, vegetable stock, or water**

2 **cups diced fresh tomatoes**

¼ **cup sliced pitted black olives**

¼ **cup chopped fresh basil or parsley,
or a combination (or more, to taste)**

Salt and freshly ground pepper to taste

Cut the chard leaves away from the stems. Trim about an inch off the bottom of
the stems, then slice them thinly. Cut the leaves into bite-size pieces or ribbons.

Heat the oil in a large steep-sided skillet or stir-fry pan. Add the onion and garlic and
sauté over medium-low heat until both are golden.

Add wine, chard leaves, and stems (in batches, if need be) until they're all in the pan.
Cover and cook over medium heat, for 2 minutes or so, until the chard is wilted and
bright green.

Stir in the tomatoes, cover; cook for 2 to 3 minutes longer, or until the chard is just
tender and the tomatoes are lightly cooked down. Stir in the olives and basil or
parsley, season with salt and pepper, and serve.

Variation
Add a cup or two of cooked cannellini beans and/or seasoned croutons.

Braised Hardy Greens with Mixed Mushrooms

4 to 6 servings

Greens and mushrooms (along with the delicious liquid created as they're soaked or cooked) are a perfect pair for braising. Even the modest amount of porcini mushrooms used here adds a substantial burst of earthy flavor.

1	ounce dried porcini mushrooms
12	ounces lacinato kale (or any kale variety), collard greens, mustard greens, or broccoli rabe
2	tablespoons extra-virgin olive oil
3	to 4 cloves garlic, minced or sliced
6	to 8 ounces mixed mushrooms (cremini, portabella, oyster mushrooms, or a combination), cleaned and sliced
2	tablespoons dry red or white wine
⅓	to ½ cup sliced sun-dried tomatoes (or oil-cured, if desired)
1	tablespoon unbleached white flour, optional
	Salt and freshly ground pepper to taste

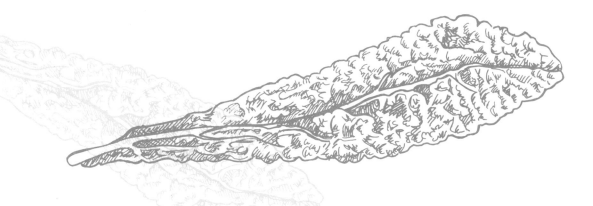

Pour ½ cup boiling water over the porcini mushrooms and let them stand until needed.

For lacinato kale and collard greens, cut leaves away from the stems. Stack a few leaves at a time; snugly roll the stacked leaves from one of the narrow ends, and slice thinly. Chop in a few places to shorten the ribbons.

For mustard greens, chop the leaves into large bite-size pieces or ribbons. For broccoli rabe, trim a half inch or so off the base of the stems, slice them into ½- to 1-inch sections, and use them for cooking, along with the stems, florets, and leaves.

Heat the oil in a large, steep-sided skillet or stir-fry pan. Add the garlic and sauté over low heat for 2 to 3 minutes, until golden.

Add the greens and cook over medium heat, stirring frequently for a minute or so.

Add the porcini and their soaking liquid, the other mushrooms, and the wine. Cover and cook for 2 minutes, until the greens are wilted down, then add the dried tomatoes. Continue to cook, stirring frequently, until the greens are tender but still nice and green.

If there is still a lot of liquid in the pan, combine the flour with just enough water to dissolve it, then drizzle this combination into the pan and cook the liquid over high heat until it has thickened. Season with salt and pepper, and serve at once.

Wine & Mustard–Braised Asian Greens

4 to 6 servings

Lest you think that stir-frying is the only technique suitable for Asian greens, braising is another way to bring out the best in this group of veggies. Thanks to my nephew, Josh Atlas, for this inspiration.

10 **to 12 ounces Asian greens (baby bok choy or any of the greens in the choy family, Chinese mustard cabbage, Chinese broccoli, or a combination)**

1 **tablespoon cornstarch**

1 **tablespoon reduced-sodium soy sauce or tamari, plus more to taste**

2 **teaspoons yellow mustard**

2 **teaspoons natural granulated sugar**

2 **tablespoons safflower or other healthy, high-heat vegetable oil**

3 **to 4 cloves garlic, minced or sliced**

3 **to 4 shallots, sliced**

¼ **cup dry white wine or sherry**

Freshly ground pepper to taste

Make sure the greens you're using are very well washed (see tips on page 12). Chop into bite-size pieces.

Combine the cornstarch in a small bowl with ¼ cup water and stir to dissolve. Add the soy sauce, mustard, and sugar and whisk together.

Heat the oil in a large steep-sided skillet or stir-fry pan. Add the garlic and shallots and sauté over low heat for 2 to 3 minutes, until golden. Add the wine and greens. Cover and cook over medium heat for just a minute or two, until the greens are just wilted.

Stir in the cornstarch mixture. Cook for just another minute or so, until the sauce thickens and the greens are tender-crisp to your liking. Season with pepper and additional soy sauce if desired, then serve at once.

Variation
This is also good with regular mustard greens.

Citrus-Braised Escarole or Mustard Greens with Apples & Nuts

6 servings

The pleasantly bitter flavor of escarole or the sharp tang of mustard greens is tempered with sweet red onions and the fruity flavors of apple and orange.

- ¼ cup pine nuts or slivered almonds
- 1 tablespoon olive oil
- 1 large red onion, quartered and thinly sliced
- 2 medium crisp, sweet apples, peeled and thinly sliced
- 1 large head escarole or mustard greens, cut into narrow ribbons
- ¼ to ⅓ cup orange juice, preferably fresh
- 2 tablespoons orange zest (from an organic orange—optional, but highly recommended)

  Salt and freshly ground pepper to taste

Heat a large skillet or stir-fry pan. Toast the pine nuts on medium-low heat until golden brown. Set aside in a small bowl.

Heat the oil in the same pan. Add the onion and sauté over medium-low heat until golden.

Add the apples and continue to sauté for about 3 minutes until slightly softened.

Add the greens in batches, then drizzle in the orange juice. Cover and cook the greens until they're just wilted down, then turn the heat up to medium-high. Cook no longer than 5 minutes, stirring frequently, until the greens are tender-crisp.

Stir in the zest, if you're using it, and season the greens with salt and pepper. Stir in the pine nuts, and serve at once.

Indian-Style Mustard Greens with Spinach

4 to 6 servings

This is a simple rendition of a popular Indian dish called *saag,* in which mild spinach acts as a counterpoint to the sharper flavor of the mustard greens. If you like your greens sharp, you'll love this dish.

1   **head mustard greens, stemmed, washed, and chopped (about 10 to 12 ounces)**

8   **ounces spinach, any variety, washed, long stems removed, and chopped (or use rinsed whole baby spinach leaves)**

1   **tablespoon olive oil or other healthy vegetable oil**

1   **to 2 teaspoons whole cumin seeds (see note)**

3   **to 4 cloves garlic, minced**

1   **to 2 teaspoons minced fresh or jarred ginger**

3   **to 4 scallions, white and green parts, sliced**

    Lemon or lime juice to taste

    Salt and freshly ground pepper to taste

Prepare the greens, as directed, before starting, since this dish comes together very quickly.

Heat the oil in a large, steep-sided skillet or stir-fry pan. Add the cumin seeds, garlic, ginger, and white parts of the scallions and sauté over medium heat, stirring for 2 to 3 minutes or until the garlic and the white parts of the scallion are golden.

Add the mustard greens in batches until they're all in, stirring continuously. Add the green parts of the scallions and ¼ to ⅓ cup water, depending on the amount of greens.

Cover and cook over medium heat until the mustard greens have just lost their raw quality, about 3 minutes. Stir the spinach into the pan in batches and cook, stirring, just until it's wilted and both greens are barely tender. (The less you cook this dish, the tastier it is, so be sure to remove the greens from the heat once they're wilted.) Add lemon or lime juice, season with salt and pepper, and serve at once.

NOTE: Whole cumin seeds are surprisingly easy to find; many well-stocked supermarkets carry them in the spice section. If you can't find them or prefer not to use them, sprinkle in 1 to 2 teaspoons of ground cumin once all the mustard greens are in the pan.

Variations

For a spicier dish, add 1 or 2 small seeded and minced fresh hot chilies at the same time as the garlic, ginger, and scallions.

Try this recipe with other bitter or sharp greens contrasted with milder ones, such as escarole and chard, or broccoli rabe and chard.

SAUCES FOR SIMPLY COOKED GREENS

"Mustard Greens" Sauce

About ½ cup, enough for 12 to 14 ounces cooked greens

This simple sweet and pungent glaze makes leafy greens (as well as other green veggies) sing. A little goes a long way, hence the modest yield.

- ¼ cup agave nectar
- ¼ cup yellow mustard
- 1 tablespoon extra-virgin olive oil
- 1 tablespoon balsamic or apple cider vinegar

Combine the ingredients in a small bowl and whisk together. Stir into greens that are just wilted and ready to serve.

Tahini-Lemon Sauce

About 1 cup, enough for 12 to 16 ounces cooked greens

This easy-to-make sauce is delicious on Simple Garlicky Greens (page 40) or steamed or wilted greens (see Simply Steaming or Wilting Greens, page 37).

- ⅓ cup tahini
- Juice of 1 to 1½ large lemons
- 2 tablespoons reduced-sodium soy sauce or tamari
- 2 tablespoons agave nectar or maple syrup
- ⅓ cup water

Place all the ingredients in a small bowl and whisk together. Stir into the nearly done greens.

Spicy Peanut or Cashew Sauce

About 1 cup, enough for 12 to 16 ounces cooked greens

This rich, spicy sauce is great on just about any variety of greens. Try it with any preparation of steamed or wilted greens (see Simply Steaming or Wilting Greens (page 37), Simple Garlicky Greens (page 40), or Basic Stir-Fried Asian Greens (page 68).

1 tablespoon olive oil or other healthy vegetable oil

2 cloves garlic, minced

2 scallions, white and green parts, sliced

2 medium tomatoes, diced

1 fresh hot chili pepper, seeded and minced
 (or other spicy seasoning like dried hot red pepper flakes
 or Thai red chili paste, to taste)

½ cup natural-style chunky peanut butter or cashew butter

1 tablespoon reduced-sodium soy sauce or tamari

1 teaspoon natural granulated sugar

Heat the oil in a large skillet. Add the garlic and the white parts of the scallions, and sauté over medium-low heat until the garlic begins to turn golden. Add the tomatoes, chili pepper, and green parts of the scallion. Cover and cook just until the tomatoes have softened, 2 to 3 minutes.

Add the peanut butter, soy sauce, and sugar. Once the peanut butter starts to soften from the heat, stir in with the tomato mixture and add a small amount of water, just enough to make this a medium-thick sauce. Stir into nearly done greens.

Avocado-Tahini Dressing

**This dressing makes about 1½ cups,
enough for 12 to 16 ounces of cooked greens, plus extra.**

Pour this delicious and decidedly rich sauce over steamed or wilted greens (see Simply Steaming or Wilting Greens, page 37), Simple Garlicky Greens (page 40), or any salad of raw greens. It's also particularly good as a dressing for massaged kale salads (see pages 146 to 153).

- 1 medium ripe avocado, peeled and diced
- ⅓ cup tahini (sesame paste)
  Juice of 1 lemon
- ½ teaspoon ground cumin
- 2 to 4 tablespoons minced fresh parsley or cilantro, to taste

Combine all the ingredients in a food processor and puree until smooth. Add ¼ to ½ cup of water, as needed, to achieve a medium-thick consistency.

Stir ½ to 1 cup of the sauce into greens once they're done. Transfer the rest to a covered container and refrigerate. Use within 3 days.

STIR-FRYING ASIAN GREENS: THE BASICS

Some Asian greens can be eaten both cooked and raw (such as regular and baby bok choy, mizuna, and tatsoi). Others, like Chinese mustard cabbage, Chinese broccoli, and some of the choy vegetables taste better lightly cooked, so stir-frying is the ideal way to prepare them.

Wash greens very well, following the tips on page 12. Taking particular care is important, especially when greens are purchased from an Asian market, since they don't get regular showers, like supermarket greens, and can be somewhat muddy.

Let the greens air-dry on a couple layers of clean kitchen towels, or dry them in a salad spinner. Although they don't need to be perfectly dry, they'll come out more crisp if they don't have a lot of water clinging to them.

Once the greens are dry and ready to go, heat enough oil to coat a stir-fry pan or wok. Safflower or another high-heat oil works well. Extra-virgin olive oil somehow doesn't suit Asian greens. Add chopped garlic and/or shallots to your liking and cook over medium heat for a minute or so. If you'd like to add any other flavorings like minced garlic or chopped chilies, now is the time to do it.

Turn the heat up to high and quickly add as many of the clean greens as will comfortably fit in the pan, stirring continuously as you add the rest. Don't overcrowd the pan, or some greens will become overcooked while others are just getting started. About a pound is tops; 12 ounces or so is easier to work with.

Sprinkle in about a quarter teaspoon of salt just as soon as all the greens are in, since this will help retain their bright green color.

Continue to stir-fry the greens for 3 minutes or so, or until they're just tender-crisp and bright green. Remove from the heat and serve at once.

CLASSIC STIR-FRIES

Basic Stir-Fried Asian Greens

6 servings

Use this basic recipe to prepare bok choy (and all other choys, many of which are listed on page 17), Chinese broccoli, Chinese mustard cabbage, mizuna, and tatsoi. It is just as perfect for preparing one type of green as it is for any combination of greens, since all of them cook down very quickly and at about the same rate.

  2 **tablespoons safflower or other high-heat oil**

  1 **small onion or 3 to 4 shallots, finely chopped**

10 **to 14 ounces any variety of Asian greens
    or a combination of greens (see suggestions above)**

  2 **to 4 cloves garlic, minced**

  1 **to 2 teaspoons grated fresh ginger (or more, to taste)**

 ½ **teaspoon natural granulated sugar**

    Salt and freshly ground black pepper to taste

  1 **teaspoon dark sesame oil, optional**

Heat the oil in a wok or stir-fry pan. Add the onion or shallots and the garlic, and sauté over medium-low heat until golden.

Quickly stir in the greens to coat them with the oil, then turn the heat up to high. Stir-fry for a minute or so, then add the ginger, sugar, and a sprinkling of salt.

Continue to stir-fry until the greens are tender-crisp, just another minute or two longer. Season with salt and pepper and drizzle in the sesame oil for extra flavor, if desired. Serve at once.

Variations

Use any or all of these. Stir-fry them briefly before adding the greens:

- 4 to 6 ounces mushrooms, any variety, cleaned and sliced
- 1 cup baby corn
- 1 medium red or yellow bell pepper, cut into long, narrow strips
- 2 to 3 cups shredded napa cabbage

Stir-Fried Bok Choy & Snow Peas
with Shiitake Mushrooms

4 to 6 servings

Serve this quick, tasty stir-fry on its own or over rice or quinoa.

1 tablespoon safflower or other healthy vegetable oil

1 medium onion, halved and sliced

1 tablespoon dark sesame oil

1 medium bunch regular bok choy
   or 4 to 6 baby bok choy, sliced diagonally, leaves chopped

4 to 6 ounces fresh shiitake mushrooms,
   stemmed and sliced

2 cups snow peas, trimmed and cut in half

2 tablespoons reduced-sodium soy sauce or tamari

3 tablespoons dry sherry

1 to 2 teaspoons grated fresh or jarred ginger

   Dried hot red pepper flakes, to taste, optional

Heat the oil in a large skillet or wok. Add the onion and stir-fry over medium heat until translucent.

Drizzle in the sesame oil and turn the heat up to high. Add the bok choy, shiitakes, snow peas, soy sauce, sherry, and ginger. Stir-fry until the vegetables are tender-crisp. Err on the side of less time than more; this takes only 2 to 3 minutes.

Add dried hot pepper flakes if desired. Season with additional soy sauce if desired and serve at once.

Stir-Fried Sesame Kale & Red Cabbage

6 servings

The trick to this pretty stir-fry is to stop the stir-fry process just shy of when you think you need to, so that both the cabbage and the kale retain their bright color.

- 8 **to 12 ounces kale, any variety**
- ½ **small head or ⅓ medium head red cabbage**
- 1½ **tablespoons olive oil**
- 1 **medium red onion, quartered and thinly sliced**
- 2 **teaspoons grated fresh or jarred ginger**
- 1 **tablespoon dark sesame oil**
- 1 **to 2 tablespoons sesame seeds (preferably unhulled)**
- **Salt and freshly ground pepper to taste**

Strip the kale leaves from the stems. Stack a few leaves and cut them into narrow strips. If desired, slice the stems thinly to use in the stir-fry; otherwise discard.

Cut the red cabbage into thin slices about 2 inches long.

Heat the olive oil in a stir-fry pan or large skillet. Add the onion and sauté over medium heat until golden and soft.

Add the ginger, kale, and cabbage. Turn the heat up to high and stir-fry for 3 to 4 minutes, stirring frequently, until both are brightly colored and tender-crisp.

Remove from the heat. Stir in the dark sesame oil and the sesame seeds. Season with salt and pepper and serve at once.

Variations

You can add a small amount of another vegetable or two to this simple veggie combination, depending on what you have on hand. Use any of the following, adding them at the same time as the kale and cabbage.

- 1 medium red bell pepper, cut into long narrow strips
- 1 cup fresh or frozen corn kernels (thawed)
- 8 to 10 baby carrots, quartered lengthwise

To spice up this recipe or its variations, add a spicy condiment such as minced fresh hot chilies or dried hot red pepper flakes, to taste.

Mustard greens are another excellent variation. You don't need to strip the leaves off the stems, just slice the leaves crosswise into long ribbons or chop into bite-size pieces. Note that mustard greens get done quickly with this stir-fry method, so take care not to overdo the cooking.

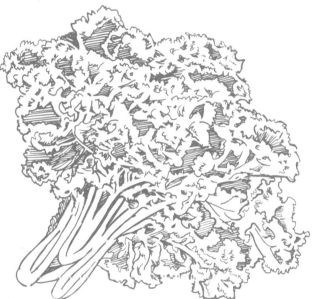

Spring Greens Stir-Fry

4 servings

This stir-fry mingles tender Asian and Western greens. Once you've prepped all the veggies, this delectable mélange is done in a flash. If you have access to a farmers' market or belong to a CSA, look for fresh ramps or garlic scapes and add them to this dish—they'll add a lovely touch of spring. If they're not available, substitute finely chopped garlic for the ramps.

       Several ramps (wild leeks) or garlic scapes (the green shoots of young garlic bulbs)

1 **bunch Chinese broccoli or broccolini, bottoms trimmed, and cut crosswise into 1-inch segments**

3 **to 4 ounces leafy spring greens (baby spinach, arugula, or an Asian green such as tatsoi or baby bok choy or other choys, or a combination of these greens)**

1½ **tablespoons olive oil**

1 **to 2 medium baby bok choy, thinly sliced**

½ **head radicchio, thinly sliced**

2 **spring onions or scallions, thinly sliced**

1 **teaspoon dark sesame oil**

       Splash of orange, lemon, or lime juice

       Salt and freshly ground pepper to taste

If you're using ramps, trim away the bulb, then cut the white part into ½-inch sections and cut the green parts and leaves thinly.

If you're using scapes, cut them into 1-inch sections.

If you're using spinach or arugula, rinse and trim the larger stems.

If you're using tatsoi, simply rinse the leaves.

If using baby bok choy, cut the stalks and leaves into thick slices crosswise.

Heat the oil in a stir-fry pan. Add the ramps and the broccoli or broccolini, and stir-fry over medium-high heat just until the broccolini is bright green, about 3 minutes.

Add the leafy greens, bok choy, and radicchio, and scallions. Continue to stir-fry 1 to 2 minutes longer, until the more tender greens are wilted and brightly colored.

Remove the pan from the heat. Stir in the sesame oil and add a splash of citrus juice, just enough to moisten the mixture. Season with salt and pepper, and serve warm or at room temperature.

Variation

Use a small amount of dandelion greens in place of or in addition to the suggested greens. If you are using bigger, somewhat tougher dandelion greens, blanch them as directed on page 38 to remove some of the bitterness.

Stir-Fried Chard with Napa Cabbage

6 servings

Napa cabbage is a superb companion to dark leafy greens, adding a lighter texture and flavor as well as visual interest. This dish comes very close to being downright addictive.

10 to 12 ounces chard, any variety, stemmed and cut into ribbons
½ medium head napa cabbage, cut into ribbons
2 tablespoons olive or other healthy vegetable oil
3 to 4 shallots, finely chopped
2 to 4 cloves garlic, minced
1 medium leek, chopped and well washed, optional
Salt and freshly ground black pepper to taste
Dried hot red pepper flakes to taste

Prepare the greens as directed before starting.

Heat the oil in a wok or stir-fry pan. Add the shallots, the garlic, and the leek, if you're using it, and sauté over medium-low heat until all are golden.

Quickly stir in the chard to coat it with the oil, then turn the heat up to high. Stir-fry for a minute or so, then add the napa cabbage. Continue to stir-fry until both are tender-crisp, about 2 to 3 minutes.

Season with salt, pepper, and dried hot red pepper flakes, and serve at once.

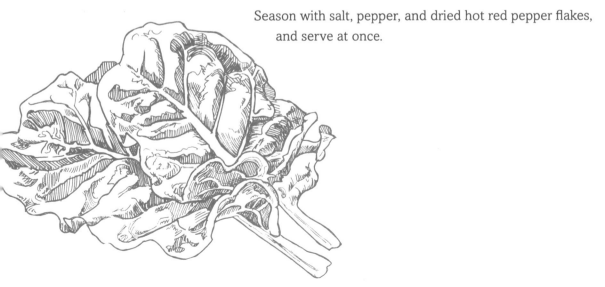

SEARED BABY BOK CHOY

Baby bok choy is at its best in the spring when it's plump and fresh. Here's a super-quick way to prepare and show it off in all its glory, both visually and in terms of flavor.

Cut each baby bok choy in half so that the widest part is exposed (leave the stem end intact). Heat just enough olive oil to coat the bottom of a large pan. When a drop of water sizzles in the pan the oil is ready. Place the bok choy halves, cut side down, on the skillet. Cover and cook them over high (but not the highest) heat for 3 minutes or until the bok choy is nicely browned. Serve with a sprinkling of salt and pepper.

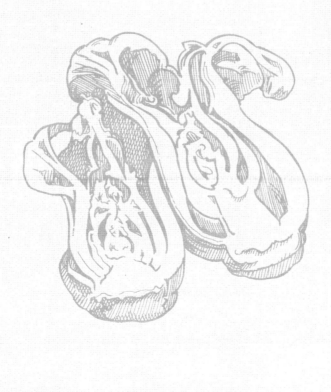

Stir-Fried Collard Greens with Variations

4 to 6 servings

Asian greens aren't the only greens that work well with the stir-fry method. Collards are quite delicious prepared this way, contrary to the conventional wisdom that collards need to be cooked or boiled for a fairly long time in order to tenderize them. You can use this basic preparation as a takeoff point for your own ideas.

10 **to 12 ounces collard greens**

1½ **tablespoons olive oil or other healthy vegetable oil**

2 **to 3 cloves garlic, minced**

2 **to 3 shallots, chopped, optional**

1 **tablespoon apple cider vinegar, or to taste, optional**

    Salt and freshly ground pepper to taste

Cut the collard leaves neatly away from the stems with kitchen shears. Stack 5 or 6 leaves that are roughly the same size on top of each other. Starting from one of the narrow ends, snugly roll up the leaves, then slice them thinly. Chop the slices in a few places to shorten the ribbons. Set them aside.

Heat the oil in a skillet or stir-fry pan. Add the garlic and optional shallots and sauté over low heat until they just start to turn golden.

Add the collard greens and a small amount of water (just enough to keep the skillet moist); turn up the heat to medium-high and cook for 3 to 4 minutes, stirring frequently, until the greens are bright and tender-crisp. Drizzle in the optional vinegar, season with salt and pepper, and serve at once.

Variations & Other Ideas

STIR-FRIED COLLARD GREENS WITH NAPA CABBAGE OR ROMAINE LETTUCE: Thinly
shred about ½ medium head napa cabbage, more or less to match the collards.
Increase the amount of oil slightly. Add the napa cabbage to the pan about 2 minutes
after the collard greens, and follow the cooking directions above. If you're using
romaine lettuce, use ½ large head or 1 small head, thinly shredded, more or less to
match the collards. Add the romaine shreds just before the collards are done. Both
the napa and romaine variations are good with a sprinkling of sesame seeds.

STIR-FRIED COLLARD GREENS WITH TOMATOES: Once the collard greens are nearly
done, add a cup or two of diced tomatoes and fresh basil and thyme. Cook for 2 to 3
minutes, or until the tomatoes have softened and are heated through.

MORE WAYS TO USE STIR-FRIED COLLARD GREENS: You can add stir-fried collard
ribbons into all sorts of vegetable mélanges, especially autumn vegetable stews
that feature orange squashes or sweet potatoes (see Hoisin-Glazed Collard Greens
& Sweet Potatoes, page 132). Stir-fried collards are also good tossed together with
cooked long noodles like soba, whose sturdy buckwheat flavor complements that
of the collard greens. Season with soy sauce or Bragg's Liquid
Aminos, and add some finely chopped scallion and/or
crushed peanuts.

OVEN-BAKED KALE CHIPS

A book on greens these days wouldn't be complete without a recipe for this trendy homemade snack. Google "kale chips recipe" and you'll get upward of a million results.

Recipes online are all over the place as far as oven temperature goes. Some suggest baking kale chips at a temperature as low as 250°F, while other aficionados go for the quick-bake method, practically roasting the leaves at 400°F. Most recipes fall in the middle and suggest baking this treat at between 300°F and 350°F. I've experimented with baking kale chips quite a bit and found the midrange to work best. Because temperature accuracy can vary from oven to oven, you might need to experiment to see which temperature works best for you. I happen to like 325°F.

For this recipe, curly green kale works best. There's no harm in trying lacinato kale (or even collard greens); they work fairly well too, but curly kale has the best crispy-crunchy mouthfeel. This is an easy recipe, but a bit of trial and error has taught me a few secrets to making kale chips come out crisp and even. Here are the basic steps:

1. Remove kale leaves from the stems and tear them into bite-size pieces—about the size of large potato chips.

2. Rinse the kale and—this is extremely important—let it dry completely. Damp kale will make soggy chips that don't bake evenly (I learned this the hard way). Use a salad spinner, or spread the kale on kitchen towels and let it dry completely.

3. Once the kale is completely dry, preheat the oven to the desired temperature (325°F works best for me).

4. Transfer the kale to a bowl and drizzle in a little olive oil. Massage it evenly into the leaves with your hands (you'll be doing more of this in chapter 3, when you make raw kale salads). At this point, if you like, you can add a tiny bit of red wine vinegar and a pinch or two of such seasonings as chili powder, cumin, smoked paprika, Cajun seasoning, or salt-free all-purpose seasoning. Don't use salt at this point, since it can make the chips soggy. Nutritional yeast, however, is a delicious flavoring that perfectly complements these chips and makes them a great source of calcium, as well as vitamin B-12. (This is especially valuable to vegans.)

5. Spread the kale in a single layer on one or two parchment-lined baking pans. Bake the kale for 12 to 20 minutes, depending on your oven's temperature. Check them from time to time. The chips should be evenly dry and crisp and just barely beginning to brown.

6. Remove the pans from the oven and let them cool until they can be handled. Carefully transfer the kale chips to a serving bowl. At this point you can sprinkle in a little salt, but you may not need or want to if you've added other tasty seasonings.

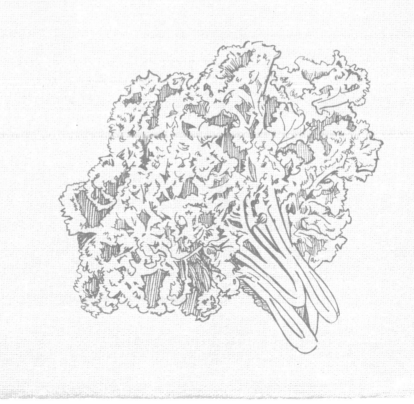

CHAPTER 2

GREENS WITH BEANS, GRAINS, PASTA & OTHER VEGETABLES

This chapter explores the wide array of greens that can be used in heartier dishes, in which they aren't quite the main attraction but play an important role. Chapter 1 showcases greens as the star of each dish. Here their role is the supportive best friend, adding flavor, texture, color, and nutrition to hearty dishes that feature grains, beans, and pasta. In addition, the greens in these recipes pair deliciously with sturdy veggies like potatoes, sweet potatoes, eggplant, and squashes.

GREENS WITH GRAINS & BEANS

Quinoa with Chard & Chickpeas, 82

Balsamic-Glazed Chickpeas & Mustard Greens, 84

Quinoa with Kale, Sweet Potatoes & Pecans, 85

Quinoa with Baby Bok Choy & Asparagus, 86

Polenta or Grits with Polenta & Caramelized Onions, 87

Bok Choy Fried Rice, 88

Dilled Spinach Rice, 90

Lemony Wild Rice with Greens, Pine Nuts & Raisins, 91

Black Rice with Black-Eyed Peas & Greens, 92

Persian Spinach with Black-Eyed Peas & Herbs, 95

Spicy Collard Greens with Black-Eyed Peas, 96

Southwestern-Style Greens with Pinto Beans, 105

Curried Sweet Potatoes with Chard & Chickpeas, 106

Collard-Wrapped Yellow Rice & Black Bean Enchiladas, 108

Tostadas with Chili-Spiced Greens & Potatoes, 110

Ragout of Broccoli Rabe with White Beans & Porcini Mushrooms, 112

White Bean & Greens Burgers, 114

GREENS WITH PASTA & NOODLES

Pasta with Two Beans & Escarole, 116

Pasta with Asparagus, Arugula & Sun-Dried Tomatoes, 117

Pasta with Greens, Chickpeas & Olives, 118

Vietnamese-Style Bean Thread Noodles with Spinach & Napa Cabbage, 120

Pad See Ew (Thai Rice Noodles with Chinese Broccoli), 122

Hoisin-Glazed Bok Choy with Tofu & Soba Noodles, 124

SATISFYING VEGGIE COMBOS

Italian Vegetable Ragout with Chard, 126

Greens with Polenta Wedges, 128

Kale & Cabbage Colcannon, 129

Collard Ribbons with Spaghetti Squash, 130

Hoisin-Glazed Collard Greens & Sweet Potatoes, 132

Cumin-Roasted Cauliflower & Kale, 135

Garlicky Potatoes with Greens & Olives, 136

Rosemary Potatoes & Collard Greens with Vegan Sausage, 138

Smoky Potatoes with Turnip Greens, 139

Roasted Eggplant Curry with Greens & Tomatoes, 140

Quinoa with Chard & Chickpeas

4 to 6 servings

Red quinoa or a combination of regular and red quinoa harmonize beautifully with the greens and make for a pretty dish, too. You can also use a variety of chard—rainbow, Swiss, or, my personal favorite, green chard—in this dish.

1 **cup quinoa (red, yellow, or a combination), rinsed in a fine sieve**

1 **natural salt-free vegetable bouillon cube**

1 **tablespoon extra-virgin olive oil**

1 **cup cooked chickpeas**

2 **to 4 cloves garlic, minced**

10 **to 12 ounces chard, any variety, stemmed and thinly sliced (use trimmed and thinly sliced stems, if you'd like)**

3 **to 4 scallions, sliced**

1 **teaspoon ground cumin**

2 **teaspoons salt-free seasoning blend (such as Spike or Mrs. Dash)**

Salt and freshly ground pepper to taste

Combine the quinoa and bouillon cube with 2 cups water in a medium saucepan and bring to a simmer. Cover and simmer gently for 15 minutes. If you'd like the quinoa to be more tender, add ½ cup additional water and simmer until absorbed. Remove from the heat.

Meanwhile, heat the oil in a large skillet. Add the chickpeas and sauté over medium heat for 5 minutes. Add the garlic and continue to sauté until both the chickpeas and garlic are golden.

Stir in the greens and about ¼ cup water. Cover and cook until the greens are tender but still bright green, stirring frequently and adding more water as needed. When the greens are about halfway done, stir in the scallions.

Add the cooked quinoa and cumin and stir together with the greens. Season with salt and pepper; cook for 2 to 3 minutes longer and serve.

Variations
Lacinato kale or collard greens work well in this recipe. Stir-fry them separately following the instructions on page 67, then stir the kale or collards into the quinoa at the last minute.

Balsamic-Glazed Chickpeas & Mustard Greens

4 servings

This simple yet perfect pairing of savory glazed chickpeas and mustard greens was contributed by Susan Voisin, this book's photographer. Delicious!

- 1 **large bunch mustard greens (about 12 ounces)**
- 1 **large red onion, thinly sliced**
- ½ **to ⅔ cup vegetable broth, divided**
- 4 **to 6 cloves garlic, minced**
- 1 **pinch dried hot red pepper flakes**
- ¼ **cup balsamic vinegar, plus more for serving**
- 1 **teaspoon soy sauce, or to taste**
- ½ **teaspoon agave nectar or sugar**
- 2 **cups cooked or one 20-ounce can chickpeas, drained and rinsed**

Remove any large stems from the greens and discard the stems. Tear or chop the leaves into bite-size pieces.

In a deep pot or wok, cook the onion in about 2 tablespoons of vegetable broth until it has faded to pink, about 4 minutes.

Add the minced garlic and red pepper flakes and another 2 tablespoons of broth and cook, stirring, for another minute.

Add the mustard greens and remaining broth. Cook, stirring, until greens are wilted but still bright green, about 3 to 5 minutes. Remove greens and onions from the pan with a slotted spoon and place in a serving dish, leaving any liquid in the pan.

Add the balsamic vinegar, soy sauce, and agave nectar or sugar to the liquid in the pan (if there is no liquid, add 2 tablespoons additional broth). Add the chickpeas and cook, stirring, over medium heat until the liquid is reduced by about half.

Spoon the chickpeas over the greens and drizzle any sauce remaining in the pan over the top. Serve warm, and pass around any additional balsamic vinegar.

Quinoa with Kale, Sweet Potatoes & Pecans

6 servings

This sumptuous pilaf looks as great as it tastes when it's prepared with red quinoa, or a combination of red and yellow quinoa.

- 1 large sweet potato, cooked or microwaved until done but still nice and firm
- 1 cup uncooked quinoa, rinsed in a fine sieve
- 1 vegetable bouillon cube
- 2 tablespoons extra-virgin olive oil
- 1 large or 2 medium leeks, white parts only, quartered lengthwise, chopped, and well rinsed
- 8 to 12 ounces kale, any variety, stemmed and finely chopped (if you'd like to use the stems, thinly slice them)
- 2 celery stalks, finely diced
- 2 to 3 scallions, minced
- 1 teaspoon ground cumin
- ⅓ to ½ cup chopped pecans

  Salt and freshly ground pepper to taste

When the sweet potato is cool enough to handle, peel and cut it into ½-inch dice.

Combine the quinoa in a small saucepan with 2 cups water (if using red quinoa, use 2½ cups water; if you're using a combination, use 2¼ cups water) and the bouillon cube. Bring to a gentle boil, then lower the heat, cover, and simmer gently until the water is absorbed, about 15 minutes. If you'd like a more tender grain, add ½ cup water and simmer until absorbed.

Heat the oil in a large skillet or stir-fry pan. Add the leeks and sauté over medium-low heat until they're soft and golden. Add the kale and a small amount of water; cover and cook until it wilts down, about 3 minutes.

Add the celery and scallions, then stir in the cooked quinoa, sweet potato, and cumin. Stir together and cook over low heat for 5 minutes, stirring occasionally.

Stir in the pecans, season with salt and pepper, and serve.

Quinoa with Baby Bok Choy & Asparagus

6 servings

This quinoa dish is filled with spring veggies and is gently seasoned with familiar Asian flavors.

- 1 **cup quinoa (yellow, red, or a combination), rinsed in a fine sieve**
- 1 **tablespoon safflower or other healthy vegetable oil**
- 2 **to 4 cloves garlic, minced**
- 3 **or 4 baby bok choy, thinly sliced crosswise**
- 8 **ounces slender asparagus, bottoms trimmed, cut into 1- to 1½-inch lengths**
- 2 **big handfuls baby spinach or arugula, or ½ bunch watercress leaves**
- 3 **to 4 scallions, sliced**
- 1 **to 2 teaspoons minced fresh or jarred ginger, to taste**
- 1 **to 2 tablespoons rice vinegar or lemon juice, to taste**
- 1 **to 2 tablespoons reduced-sodium soy sauce**
- **Freshly ground pepper to taste**
- **Chopped peanuts or cashews for topping, optional**

Combine the quinoa in a medium saucepan with 2 cups water (use 2½ cups water for red quinoa; 2¼ cups, if you're using a combination); bring to a simmer. Cover and simmer gently for 15 minutes. If you'd like the quinoa to be more tender, add ½ cup additional water and simmer until absorbed. Remove from the heat.

Heat the oil in a stir-fry pan. Add the garlic, bok choy, and asparagus. Stir-fry over medium-high heat for 3 to 4 minutes or until tender-crisp.

Stir in the spinach and scallions and stir-fry just until the spinach wilts (this should take less than a minute.)

Add the cooked quinoa, then quickly stir in the ginger, vinegar, and soy sauce. Stir together and remove the pan from the heat. Grind in some pepper and serve at once. Pass around chopped nuts for topping, if desired.

Polenta or Grits with Spinach & Caramelized Onions

4 to 6 servings

Sometimes simple preparations are the most sublime. Here the combination of mellow grits or polenta, sweet onion, tender baby spinach, and briny olives practically melts in your mouth.

- 2 **tablespoons olive oil**
- 2 **large red onions, quartered and thinly sliced**
- 1 **cup stone-ground corn grits or coarse cornmeal (polenta)**
- 1½ **tablespoons nonhydrogenated margarine, such as Earth Balance**
  Salt to taste
- 10 **to 12 ounces baby spinach, rinsed**
- ½ **cup finely chopped pitted brine-cured black olives (such as kalamata) or sliced sun-dried tomatoes**

Heat the oil in a wide skillet. Add the onions and sauté over low heat until they're soft and lightly browned—this will take at least 20 minutes or perhaps more, depending on how soft you'd like the onions. The slower you cook them, the sweeter they'll be.

Meanwhile, bring 4 cups water to a gentle boil in a medium saucepan. Move the saucepan off the burner and turn the heat down to low. Slowly whisk in the grits, stirring constantly to avoid lumps. Cover and cook gently over low heat for 15 to 20 minutes, whisking occasionally, or until the mixture is tender and thick.

Remove the cooked grits from the heat and stir in the margarine. Season with salt.

Once the onions are caramelized, push them to one half of the skillet. Add the spinach to the other half of the skillet in batches, until you've used all the spinach, covering and cooking until it's just wilted down. Remove the skillet from the heat.

To serve, spoon the grits into individual bowls. Top with the greens, followed by a generous spoonful of the onions and a sprinkling of olives or dried tomatoes. Serve at once.

Bok Choy Fried Rice

4 to 6 servings

Here's a simple and colorful Asian-style rice mélange featuring plenty of baby bok choy. You can make it even greener by adding other tender leafy greens (see variation below).

1   **cups uncooked brown or brown basmati rice, rinsed (see note)**

1   **tablespoon olive oil**

2   **cloves garlic, minced**

4   **medium baby bok choy, stalks sliced thinly, leaves chopped**

1   **medium red bell pepper, cut into short, narrow strips**

½   **cup frozen green peas, thawed**

1   **15-ounce can baby corn, drained**

3   **to 4 scallions, white and green parts, sliced**

1   **to 2 teaspoons grated fresh or jarred ginger, to taste**

2   **teaspoons dark sesame oil**

2   **tablespoons reduced-sodium soy sauce, or to taste**

     Freshly ground pepper to taste

Combine the rice with 3½ cups water in a medium saucepan. Bring to a boil, then lower the heat. Cover the rice and simmer gently until the water is absorbed, 30 to 35 minutes.

About 10 minutes before the rice is done, heat the oil in a stir-fry pan. Add the garlic, bok choy, and bell pepper and stir-fry over medium-high heat for 2 to 3 minutes.

Add the peas, baby corn, and scallions to the pan, and continue to stir-fry for 1 to 2 minutes, just until they're heated through.

Stir in the cooked rice and ginger. Drizzle in the sesame oil and soy sauce, and stir well to combine. Continue to cook the mixture for 4 to 5 minutes longer over high heat, stirring frequently. Season with additional soy sauce and pepper, if desired, then serve.

NOTE: Although this dish works beautifully with ordinary brown rice, try making it with another variety to make it even fancier. You might try one or more of these varieties: black forbidden, Bhutanese red, or a blend of several rice varieties.

Variation

You can add a small amount of leafy greens to this dish as well—tatsoi, mizuna, baby spinach, or baby arugula are good choices. When the dish is done, just pile the greens on top, cover them for a minute or so, then stir them in the rice once they're wilted.

Dilled Spinach Rice

4 to 6 servings

This is a simple, delicious, high-fiber recipe that incorporates a generous portion of wilted spinach. Why just serve brown rice when you can make it green so easily?

- 1 **cup uncooked brown rice, rinsed**
- 1 **tablespoon olive oil**
- 2 **to 3 cloves garlic, minced**
- 12 **to 16 ounces spinach, stemmed and washed,**
  or young or baby spinach, rinsed and left whole
- 2 **to 3 scallions, chopped**
- ¼ **cup chopped fresh dill, or more, to taste**
  Juice of ½ to 1 lemon, to taste
  Salt and freshly ground pepper to taste
- 2 **tablespoons sesame seeds, optional**

Combine the rice with 2½ cups water and bring to a gentle boil. Lower the heat, cover, and simmer gently, until the water is absorbed, about 30 minutes.

Heat the oil in a small soup pot or large skillet. Add the garlic and sauté over low heat until golden. Add the spinach in batches, covering and briefly wilting until it's all in the pot. Cook until all of the spinach is just wilted, then remove it from the heat.

Drain the spinach well but don't squeeze it. Transfer it to a cutting board and chop finely.

When the rice is done, stir in the spinach, scallions, dill, and lemon juice. Season with salt and pepper, and stir in the sesame seeds, if desired. Serve at once.

Variation

Use a small portion of arugula in place of some of the spinach.

Lemony Wild Rice with Greens, Pine Nuts & Raisins

4 to 6 servings

Balancing the bitterness of winter greens with rich pine nuts and sweet raisins is an old Sicilian trick that also yields a dish that's both fortifying and fabulous. This tasty recipe was contributed by my friend Ellen Kanner.

4	**cups vegetable broth or water**
1	**cup wild rice, rinsed**
2	**tablespoons extra-virgin olive oil**
1	**large onion, chopped**
10	**to 12 ounces collards greens or kale (any variety), stemmed and sliced into narrow ribbons**
2	**organic lemons, zested and juiced**
1	**good pinch dried hot red pepper flakes**
	Salt and freshly ground pepper to taste
¼	**cup pine nuts, lightly toasted**
¼	**cup raisins, or more, to taste**

In a large saucepan or small soup pot, bring the broth or water to a boil. Add the wild rice. Cover and simmer over low heat for 30 minutes. Turn off the heat and leave the pot on the burner for another half hour or so, until all the liquid is absorbed.

In a large skillet, heat the oil over medium-high heat. Add the chopped onion and sauté for about 5 minutes, stirring until the onion softens. Add the greens, and stir quickly to coat them with the oil, then add ¼ cup water. Continue cooking until the greens are just wilted, about 3 to 5 minutes.

Add the cooked rice and stir the mixture gently to combine. Add the grated zest from both lemons; squeeze in the lemon juice; and season the mixture with red pepper flakes, salt, and pepper. Sprinkle with pine nuts and raisins just before serving.

Black Rice with Black-Eyed Peas & Greens

6 to 8 servings

An invigorating mélange of flavors, textures, and colors, this is an attractive dish to serve hot or at room temperature. I just love the way the corn, black-eyed peas, and greens look against the dark rice, but if brown rice is what you've got on hand, that will work nicely too.

- 1 **cup forbidden black rice (or wild rice), rinsed**
- 3 **cups vegetable broth or water**
- 3 **tablespoons olive oil**
- 3 **medium carrots, thinly sliced**
- 2 **large celery stalks, finely diced**
- 3 **to 4 scallions, white and green parts, thinly sliced**
- 2 **cups cooked fresh or thawed frozen corn kernels (from 3 medium-large ears)**
- 10 **to 12 ounces collards greens or kale (any variety), stemmed and cut into narrow ribbons**
- 1 **15- to 16-ounce can black-eyed peas, drained and rinsed**
- 2 **tablespoons balsamic vinegar**
  - **Juice of ½ to 1 lemon, to taste**
- ¼ **cup chopped fresh dill, or more, to taste**
- ¼ **cup chopped fresh parsley, or more, to taste**
  - **Salt and freshly ground pepper to taste**
  - **Toasted pumpkin seeds for topping, optional**

Combine the rice in a saucepan with the broth. Bring to a simmer, then cover and simmer gently until the water is absorbed, about 40 minutes.

Heat the oil in a large skillet or stir fry pan. Add the carrots, celery, and white parts of the scallion and sauté over medium heat until all are golden. Stir in the green parts of the scallion and the corn.

Stir in the greens, then add ¼ cup water. Continue cooking until greens are wilted down and nearly tender, about 3 to 5 minutes.

Add the black-eyed peas, vinegar, and lemon juice. Stir together and cook for a minute or two, then stir in the wild or black rice.

Stir in the dill and parsley, and then season with salt and pepper. Serve at once, passing around pumpkin seeds for topping individual servings, if desired.

Variation
Use stemmed and sliced turnip greens in place of all or part of the collards or kale.

GREENS WITH BEANS

Leafy greens and high-protein beans are a compatible duo, with so many ways to vary the combination.

The most basic way to prepare a simple, satisfying dish of greens and beans is to start with the recipe for Simple Garlicky Greens on page 40. When the greens are about halfway done, you can mix in cooked or drained canned beans, along with the other ingredients and seasonings, at the same time. Continue cooking the greens until they are as tender as you like and the mixture is heated through. Here are some variations on the theme, ingredients that add a distinctive, regional style to greens and bean combos:

ITALIAN: White beans, tomatoes, parsley, and basil (particularly good with chard)

INDIAN: Kidney beans or lentils, curry spices, and cilantro (a hit with spinach or mustard greens)

SOUTHWESTERN: Pinto or black beans and fresh hot or mild chili peppers or a prepared salsa (delicious with any kind of greens)

CREOLE: Black-eyed peas or small white beans, tomatoes, fresh basil, and fresh or dried thyme (especially tasty with collard greens or any variety of chard)

Persian Spinach with Black-Eyed Peas & Herbs

6 servings

Sabzi is the Persian word for the greens and herbs that are typically used in Middle Eastern cuisine. The distinct flavors of spinach and black-eyed peas, combined with sweet spices, create a delightfully offbeat dish.

- 2 tablespoons extra-virgin olive oil
- 1 large or 2 medium leeks (white and palest green parts only), chopped and well rinsed
- 14 to 16 ounces fresh spinach, stemmed and coarsely chopped, or baby spinach leaves, rinsed
- ½ cup chopped fresh parsley
- 4 scallions, sliced
- 3 to 4 cups cooked black-eyed peas, or two 16-ounce cans, drained and rinsed
- Juice of ½ to 1 lemon, to taste
- ½ teaspoon ground cinnamon
- ¼ teaspoon ground nutmeg
- Salt and freshly ground pepper to taste
- Hot cooked rice or other grain

Heat the oil in a large skillet or stir-fry pan. Add the leek and sauté for 5 to 8 minutes, or until it's limp and tender.

Add the spinach, parsley, scallions, and ¼ cup water. Cover and steam just until the spinach is wilted, then stir in the black-eyed peas, lemon juice, and spices. Cook until completely heated through, then season with salt and pepper. Serve at once over hot cooked grains.

Spicy Collard Greens with Black-Eyed Peas

4 to 6 servings as a side dish

Collard greens, black-eyed peas, and fresh tomatoes are a most companionable trio, especially when they're united by the smoky heat provided by chilies and smoked paprika. This dish is absolutely delicious served with or over cooked stone-ground grits.

10 to 14 ounces collard greens

1 tablespoon olive oil

3 to 4 shallots or 1 medium onion, minced

2 to 3 cloves garlic, minced

1 to 2 small fresh hot chili peppers, seeded and minced

2 cups diced ripe tomatoes

3 to 4 cups cooked or two 15- to 16-ounce cans black-eyed peas, drained and rinsed

1 tablespoon apple cider vinegar

Smoked paprika, to taste

Salt to taste

Cut the collard leaves neatly away from the stems with kitchen shears. Make a stack of 5 or 6 leaves that are about the same size. Snugly roll up the leaves from one of the narrow ends, then slice the roll into thin strips. Chop the strips in a few places to shorten the ribbons.

Heat the oil in a large skillet. Add the shallots or onion and sauté over medium heat until translucent. Add the garlic and chilies and continue to sauté until the onion is lightly browned.

Add the collards and just enough water to keep the bottom of the skillet moist. Turn the heat up to medium-high and cook, stirring frequently, for 3 to 4 minutes, or until the greens are bright green and tender-crisp.

Add the tomatoes, black-eyed peas, and vinegar. Continue to cook the mixture until it comes to a gentle simmer, about 3 minutes.Season with smoked paprika until the dish is as hot as you want it to be. Season with a little salt, to taste, and serve at once.

Chard with Brussels
Sprouts & Red Peppers
(page 50)

Stir-Fried Sesame Kale & Red Cabbage (page 70)

Seared Baby Bok Choy (page 75)

Curried Sweet Potatoes with Chard & Chickpeas (page 106)

Orange & Cucumber Salad with Spring Greens (page 155)

Very Green Avocado-
Tahini Dip (page 173)

Italian-Style Potato &
Escarole Soup (page 178)

Green Velvet Smoothie
with Banana & Avocado
(page 209)

Southwestern-Style Greens with Pinto Beans

4 to 6 servings

This simple, traditional preparation of pinto beans originally called for any wild greens that grew locally. Contemporary recipes for this combo call for spinach or chard instead. The dark greens in this dish look very appealing, mixed with the pink beans, and the more garlicky you make them the better.

- 1 **pound spinach or chard, any variety**
- 1½ **tablespoons extra-virgin olive oil**
- 2 **to 3 cloves garlic, minced**
- 1 **to 2 small fresh hot chili peppers**
- 3 **scallions, white and green parts, finely chopped**
- 2 **cups cooked or one 15-to 16-ounce can pinto beans, drained and rinsed**
- 1 **teaspoon ground cumin**
  Salt and freshly ground black pepper

Stem and wash the greens and coarsely chop the leaves. If you're using chard, trim away the thicker midribs from the leaves and thinly slice them. Steam the greens with a very small amount of water in a large, tightly covered soup pot until they're wilted. The spinach will be done as soon as it wilts, but the chard needs to steam a bit longer (you'll know it's done when the leaves turn a deep green). Drain the greens and finely chop them.

Heat the oil in a large skillet. Add the garlic and sauté over low heat until it just begins to turn golden. Add the scallions and sauté until they soften just a bit. Stir in the greens, beans, and seasonings. Cook the mixture, covered, over low heat for 5 minutes, or just until everything is well heated through.

Curried Sweet Potatoes with Chard & Chickpeas

4 to 6 servings

A superb fusion of flavors permeates this nourishing harvest dish. Serve it like a stew in shallow bowls, accompanied by warm flatbread.

1 tablespoon olive oil

2 to 3 cloves garlic, minced

2 large sweet potatoes or 4 medium garnet yams,
   peeled and cut into large dice

1 16- to 20-ounce can chickpeas, drained and rinsed

1 16-ounce can diced tomatoes
   (such as fire-roasted, a particularly flavorful variety)

2 scallions, thinly sliced

2 teaspoons good-quality curry powder, or more, to taste

2 teaspoons minced fresh ginger, more or less to taste

1 teaspoon ground cumin

8 to 12 ounces chard, any variety,
   or a combination of chard and beet greens

¼ cup chopped cilantro or parsley, or more or less, to taste

¼ cup raisins, optional (but highly recommended)

   Salt and freshly ground pepper to taste

Heat the oil in a large skillet or a stir-fry pan. Add the garlic and sauté over low heat until golden.

Add the sweet potato dice and about 1½ cups of water. Bring the mixture to a simmer and cook until the sweet potatoes are tender, adding just enough additional water, if needed, to keep the mixture moist as it cooks.

Stir in the chickpeas, tomatoes, scallions, curry powder, ginger, and cumin and bring the mixture to a simmer again; cook over low heat for 10 minutes or so, until the tomatoes have been reduced to a sauce and the flavors have mingled.

Meanwhile, strip or cut the chard leaves (and beet greens, if you're using them) away from the stems. Slice the stems thinly, and cut the leaves into strips.

Add the chard to the skillet, in batches if necessary, and cover. Cook briefly, just until the chard wilts, and stir it into the mixture. Cook over low heat for 5 minutes, or until the chard is tender but not overdone. Stir in the cilantro and optional raisins. Season with salt and pepper, then serve.

Variation

Stemmed, coarsely chopped mustard greens or spinach or whole baby spinach leaves can be used in place of chard, using the same directions as for the chard. If you'd like to try kale or collard greens in this dish, I'd suggest steaming (page 37) or stir-frying (page 67) these greens before adding them to the dish in the last step.

You can also vary the kind of beans in this recipe. Try black beans, red beans, or pinto beans.

Collard-Wrapped Yellow Rice
& Black Bean Enchiladas

8 to 10 generous rolls, 1 or 2 per serving

Large collard green leaves make amazing wrappers for grain and bean dishes. You can vary this recipe using other grains, such as quinoa or couscous.

8 to 10 large collard leaves

1 tablespoon extra-virgin olive oil

1 medium onion, chopped

2 to 3 cloves garlic, minced

1 medium green or red bell pepper, finely diced

2 cups cooked brown rice or other grain of your choice

1 15-to 16-ounce can black beans, drained and rinsed

1 small fresh hot chili pepper, seeded and minced,
or one 4-ounce can chopped mild green chilies

¼ cup minced fresh cilantro

1 teaspoon ground cumin

½ teaspoon dried oregano

¼ teaspoon ground turmeric

Salt and freshly ground pepper to taste

1 cup store-bought salsa (use a flavorful variety such as chipotle)

1 cup tomato sauce

Preheat the oven to 375°F.

Cut the stems from the bottom of the collard leaves. Lay them, one at a time, on a cutting board, with the protruding side of the stem facing up. Using a sharp knife, skim off part of the stem so that it is flatter. Rinse the leaves.

Bring a generous amount of water to a boil in a 4-quart soup pot. Immerse the collard greens in the water and simmer steadily for 3 minutes. Drain the leaves and let them rest in a colander.

Heat the oil in a skillet. Add the onion and sauté until it's translucent. Add the garlic and bell pepper and continue to sauté until the mixture is golden.

Add the rice, beans, chili pepper, cilantro, and seasonings. Cook over medium heat until the mixture is well heated through, about 5 minutes.

In a small mixing bowl, combine the salsa and tomato sauce and stir together. Pour half of this sauce evenly over the bottom of a shallow 9- by 13-inch baking dish.

To assemble, arrange ⅓ to ½ cup of the rice mixture on each collard leaf (depending on the size; after doing one, you'll get a sense of how much filling fits comfortably in each leaf). Fold the bottom of the leaf over the filling, then fold each side in toward the middle, and roll like a burrito.

Arrange each roll in the casserole dish, and once they're all in, spoon the remaining sauce over them. Cover the casserole dish with foil.

Bake 40 to 45 minutes, or until a fork can be easily inserted into one of the rolls. Serve at once.

Tostadas with Chili-Spiced Greens & Potatoes

8 tostadas

This delectable recipe was inspired by my friend Helen Gutfriend. With its Southwestern flair, it is a great dish to serve with a side of refried beans and a simple salad.

6 medium potatoes

8 corn tortillas

2 tablespoons extra-virgin olive oil

1 medium onion, finely chopped

3 to 4 cloves garlic, minced

8 to 10 ounces greens (any variety of kale, chard, spinach, or turnip greens, or a combination), stemmed and chopped

1 to 2 small fresh green chili peppers, seeded and minced, or one 4-ounce can mild chopped green chilies

1 medium ripe avocado, well mashed

1 cup salsa verde

Juice of ½ to 1 lime, to taste

1 to 2 teaspoons ground cumin, to taste

Salt and freshly ground pepper to taste

1 red bell pepper, cut into very thin strips

¼ to ½ cup minced fresh cilantro, optional

Bake, cook, or microwave the potatoes ahead of time until they're done but still firm. When the potatoes are cool enough to handle, peel and slice them.

Preheat the oven to 375°F.

Spread the tortillas on a baking sheet and place it in the center of the preheated oven. Bake the tortillas for 10 minutes, or until they're crisp and dry, then remove them from the oven.

Meanwhile, heat the oil in a large skillet. Add the onion and sauté over medium heat until it's translucent. Add the garlic and continue to sauté until the onion is golden.

Add the greens and chili peppers, stirring quickly to coat them with the oil; sauté the greens until they're wilted and just tender.

Add the potatoes, avocado, salsa, lime juice, and cumin, and stir together gently. Cook until the mixture is well heated through. Season with salt and pepper.

To serve, divide the potato and greens mixture evenly among the crisp corn tortillas, allowing 1 or 2 tortillas per serving. Garnish the top of each tostada with a little red bell pepper and cilantro and serve at once.

Ragout of Broccoli Rabe with White Beans & Porcini Mushrooms

6 servings

This earthy preparation is good enough to be served on its own with a hunk of crusty bread, but it's just as delicious served over pasta or polenta.

- 1 ounce dried porcini mushrooms
- 8 to 12 ounces broccoli rabe
- 2 tablespoons olive oil
- 3 to 4 cloves garlic, minced
- 2 to 3 shallots, minced
- ¼ cup dry red wine
- 1 15- to 16-ounce can cannellini (large white beans)
- 1 15- to 16-ounce can diced tomatoes, with liquid (preferably Italian-style or fire-roasted)
- ½ cup pitted cured black olives, halved
- 2 tablespoons unbleached white flour
- ¼ cup minced fresh parsley
  Salt and freshly ground pepper to taste

Place the porcini in a heatproof bowl and cover them with 1 cup boiling water. Let them stand until they're needed.

Trim about an inch off the bottoms of the broccoli rabe stalks, then cut them into about 2-inch sections.

Heat the oil in a deep skillet or stir-fry pan. Add the garlic and shallots and sauté until golden.

Add the broccoli rabe, wine, and ½ cup water. Cover and cook the greens until they're bright green, then add the mushrooms and their liquid, followed by the beans, tomatoes, and olives. Bring the liquid to a simmer, then cover and simmer the mixture gently for 5 minutes, or until the broccoli rabe is tender but still retains its color.

In a bowl, combine the flour with just enough water to dissolve it and whisk the mixture until it's smooth. Pour the mixture into the skillet and stir it in to thicken the liquid.

Stir in the parsley, and season the mixture with salt and pepper. Serve the ragout at once.

Variations

Try substituting kale for the broccoli rabe. Use a good-size bunch of kale, about 10 to 12 ounces, stemmed and chopped into bite-size pieces. Or if you'd like to stay with a pleasantly bitter taste, use a medium head of escarole, cut into shreds.

White Bean & Greens Burgers

12 burgers

A mild yet flavorful burger, this toothsome combination of beans and greens is equally good eaten as a sandwich—in a pita, on a roll, or with English muffins—as it is with no bread at all.

- ⅓ **cup quick-cooking oats or quinoa flakes**
- 1 **tablespoon olive oil, plus more for cooking burgers**
- 1 **medium onion, chopped**
- 2 **to 3 cloves garlic, minced**
- 4 **to 6 ounces greens (baby or regular spinach, kale, or any variety of chard), stemmed, rinsed well, and coarsely chopped**
- 2 **cups cooked or one 15- to 16-ounce can cannellini or great northern beans, drained and rinsed**
- 2 **scallions, minced**
- 1 **tablespoon minced fresh dill, or 1 teaspoon dried**
- 1 **teaspoon salt-free all-purpose seasoning blend (such as Spike or Mrs. Dash)**
- ¼ **cup wheat germ or fine breadcrumbs**

  Salt and freshly ground pepper to taste

Combine the oats with ⅔ cup boiling water in a small bowl. Let stand until needed.

Heat the oil in a medium skillet. Add the onion and sauté over medium heat until translucent. Add the garlic and continue to sauté until the onion is golden.

Add the greens of your choice and 2 to 3 tablespoons of water for greens other than spinach. Cover and cook until the greens are wilted down but still nice and green. This will take less than a minute for spinach, 3 to 4 minutes for chard, and 3 to 5 minutes for kale. Remove the skillet from the heat.

In a food processor, combine the greens mixture with the remaining ingredients, as well as the cooked oatmeal. Pulse on and off until the mixture is coarsely and evenly chopped, not pureed.

Heat just enough oil to coat the bottom of a large, nonstick skillet. When it is sizzling-hot, ladle ¼-cup portions of the mixture onto the skillet and flatten lightly into to 3- to 4-inch rounds. As you cook the burgers in batches, fry them on both sides over medium heat until they're nicely browned. Drain cooked burgers on paper towels and keep them warm while you cook the rest of the batch.

Serve the burgers warm or at room temperature, with or without bread.

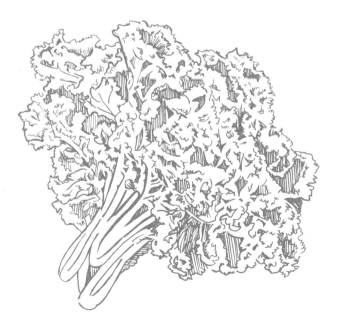

GREENS WITH PASTA & NOODLES

Pasta with Two Beans & Escarole

6 servings

Pasta, beans, and greens comprise a classic trio in Italian cuisine. It's easy to see why—the combination is healthful and hearty. The slight bitterness of the escarole is tempered by cooking it lightly. Try this recipe with broccoli rabe; it's delicious too.

- 8 **ounces fusilli or rotini**
- 3 **tablespoons extra-virgin olive oil**
- 1 **medium onion, chopped, or 3 to 4 shallots, sliced**
- 3 **to 4 cloves garlic, minced**
- ½ **large head escarole, well washed, and cut into ½-inch-wide strips**
- 1 **heaping cup cooked or canned (drained and rinsed) cannellini (large white beans)**
- 1 **heaping cup cooked or canned (drained and rinsed) red or pink beans**
- ¼ **cup sun-dried tomatoes, cut into strips, or more, to taste**

  Sliced fresh basil leaves to taste

  Salt and freshly ground pepper to taste

Cook the pasta in plenty of rapidly simmering water until *al dente,* then drain.

Meanwhile, heat about half of the oil in a large wide skillet. Add the onion and garlic and sauté over medium-low heat until golden, then add the escarole. Add enough water to keep the bottom of the skillet moist, then cover and cook for about 4 to 5 minutes, until the escarole is tender-crisp, stirring once or twice.

Stir in the beans and dried tomatoes. Cook the mixture over low heat until everything is well heated through, about 4 to 5 minutes longer.

Combine the cooked pasta with the mixture from the skillet in a large serving bowl and toss together. Drizzle in the remaining olive oil, season with salt and pepper, and toss again. Serve at once.

Pasta with Asparagus, Arugula & Sun-Dried Tomatoes

4 servings

Here's a simple, light pasta dish that features two spring vegetables—and it's ready in the time it takes to cook the pasta.

10	to 12 ounces pasta, any short shape
10	to 12 ounces fresh asparagus
2	tablespoons extra-virgin olive oil, plus more, as desired
2	to 3 cloves garlic, minced
6	to 8 ounces fresh arugula leaves, rinsed
½	cup sliced sun-dried tomatoes, oil cured or not, as you prefer
¼	cup minced fresh parsley, or more, to taste
	Salt and freshly ground pepper to taste

Cook the pasta in plenty of rapidly simmering water, until *al dente,* then drain.

Meanwhile, trim the woody ends from the asparagus spears and scrape off any tough skin with a vegetable peeler. (Fresh slender spring asparagus usually needs no scraping.) Cut the spears into 1- to 2-inch long pieces and set aside.

Heat the oil in a small skillet and add the garlic. Sauté over low heat for a minute or two or until the garlic is golden. Add the asparagus and a small amount of water. Cover and steam until the asparagus is done to your liking, but still bright green. Add the arugula, cover, and steam very briefly (less than a minute will do), just until the arugula wilts down slightly.

Combine the pasta, asparagus, and arugula mixture, dried tomatoes, and parsley in a serving bowl and toss well. Drizzle in a little extra olive oil, if you'd like. Season with salt and pepper and serve at once.

Variation
Substitute baby spinach for the arugula or use half of each. Or use a portion of tatsoi, mizuna, or young dandelion greens in place of the arugula.

Pasta with Greens, Chickpeas & Olives

4 to 6 servings

All you need is a salad and some crusty bread to accompany this hearty pasta dish, which abounds with greens of your choice.

10 to 12 ounces rotini, rotelle, or cavatappi (spiral pasta)

10 to 12 ounces chard, kale, or spinach, any variety

2 tablespoons extra-virgin olive oil

2 to 3 cloves garlic, minced

1 small red bell pepper, cut into strips

3 medium ripe tomatoes, diced

1 15- to 16-ounce can chickpeas, drained and rinsed

½ cup sliced pitted oil-cured olives (such as kalamatas)

1 tablespoon fresh oregano leaves or 1 teaspoon dried oregano

Salt and freshly ground pepper to taste

¼ to ½ teaspoon dried hot red pepper flakes, optional

¼ cup lightly toasted pine nuts, optional

Cook the pasta in plenty of rapidly simmering water until *al dente,* then drain and transfer to a large serving bowl.

If you're using any variety of chard, cut the leaves away from the stems and chop them coarsely or cut them into ribbons. If you plan to use the stems from chard, trim an inch or so away from the bottom, then slice thinly. If you're using kale, strip the leaves from the stems, and cut them into narrow ribbons or small bite-size pieces. Thinly slice the stems if you plan to use them; otherwise, discard them. Stem larger spinach leaves and chop coarsely; if you're using baby spinach, use the leaves whole.

Heat the oil in a large skillet. Add the garlic and bell pepper and sauté over medium heat until the garlic is lightly golden and the bell pepper softens, about 3 minutes.

Add the greens and stir in quickly to coat them with the oil. If you're using spinach, cover and let it wilt for 30 seconds or so. If you're using kale or collards, add a couple tablespoons of water, cover, and cook the greens for 2 to 3 minutes, until they're just wilted and bright green.

Add the tomatoes, chickpeas, olives, and oregano. Stir together and cook the mixture for 3 to 4 minutes, stirring frequently until everything is heated through.

Combine the mixture from the skillet with the pasta in the serving bowl and toss together. Season it with salt, pepper, and red pepper flakes, if you like. Sprinkle the optional pine nuts over the pasta, and serve.

Vietnamese-Style Bean-Thread Noodles with Spinach & Napa Cabbage

4 servings

This pleasingly offbeat, Westernized rendition of a Vietnamese noodle dish makes good use of the pleasant synergy of dark greens and napa cabbage.

4 ounces bean-thread (cellophane) noodles

2 tablespoons vegetable oil

1 large onion, quartered and thinly sliced

2 cloves garlic, minced

4 heaping cups thinly shredded napa cabbage

2 heaping cups diced fresh tomatoes

1 cup fresh mung bean sprouts

8 ounces spinach, any variety, stemmed, if leaves are large; or baby spinach leaves, whole

8 ounces firm tofu, diced

2 to 3 tablespoons rice vinegar, to taste

Dried hot red pepper flakes to taste

Salt to taste

Chopped peanuts for garnish, optional

Thinly sliced fresh basil leaves for garnish, optional

Combine the noodles with enough hot water to cover them in a heatproof container. Let them soak, covered, for about 20 minutes, or until done but still firm. Drain the noodles, then place them on a cutting board and chop in several directions to shorten.

Meanwhile, heat the oil in a stir-fry pan. Add the onion and stir-fry over medium heat until translucent. Turn up the heat, add the garlic and cabbage and stir-fry until the cabbage is tender-crisp and lightly browned, about 5 to 7 minutes.

Add the tomatoes and sprouts and continue to fry, stirring frequently, until the tomatoes are soft and the sprouts tender-crisp, another 5 to 7 minutes.

Add the spinach to the pan and cover; cook just until it wilts.

Stir in the tofu, vinegar, red pepper flakes, and noodles. Cook, stirring, just until everything is well heated through, then season with salt. Serve at once, garnishing each serving with some chopped peanuts and basil, if desired.

Variation

Use tatsoi and/or mizuna in place of some or all of the spinach. Or use chard in place of spinach.

Pad See Ew (Thai Rice Noodles with Chinese Broccoli)

6 servings

This delicious Thai-style noodle dish is usually made with Chinese broccoli (gai lan), which isn't easy to find. A combination of broccolini and baby spinach makes an excellent substitute. Using rombi or another wide, flat pasta works well, though the dish is more authentic with wide rice noodles. Narrower rice noodles, such as those used for pad thai, are easier to find in natural foods stores and supermarkets than the wide rice noodles, so the former will do as well. Despite the various steps and (sorry!) three different cooking vessels, this dish comes together within 30 minutes.

FOR THE SAUCE:

⅓ cup reduced-sodium soy sauce or tamari

2 tablespoons black bean sauce (look for this in the Asian food section of well-stocked supermarkets)

3 tablespoons natural granulated sugar

8 ounces extra-wide rice noodles (or substitute pad thai rice noodles or any wide, flat noodle like rombi)

1 14- to 16-ounce tub extra-firm tofu

3 tablespoons safflower or other high-heat vegetable oil

3 to 4 cloves garlic, minced

8 to 12 ounces Chinese broccoli (gai lan) carefully washed, or see variations

1 14-ounce can baby corn, drained

3 to 4 scallions, white and green parts, sliced

4 ounces baby bella mushrooms, stemmed, cleaned, and halved, optional

Freshly ground pepper to taste

Combine the ingredients for the sauce in a small bowl and stir together. Set aside.

Cook the noodles according to package directions. Make sure to follow directions precisely for rice noodles; otherwise they cook into a sticky mush. When done, drain the noodles.

Cut the tofu into 6 slabs crosswise and blot very well between layers of paper towels. Cut each slab into 2 squares, then cut each square on the diagonal into 4 small triangles. If that's totally confusing, simply dice the tofu.

Heat 2 tablespoons of the oil in a stir-fry pan or wok. Add the tofu and sauté over medium-high heat, stirring frequently, until nicely golden brown on most sides. Remove to a plate and set aside until needed.

Heat the remaining oil in the stir-fry pan. Add the garlic and sauté over low heat for 2 to 3 minutes, until golden.

Trim about an inch off the bottoms of the Chinese broccoli stems, then cut them crosswise into 1½- to 2-inch pieces. Chop the floret sections coarsely. Add them to the stir-fry pan along with the baby corn, scallions, and mushrooms, if you're using them. Stir-fry the mixture for about 2 minutes, or until the broccoli is tender-crisp.

Stir in the cooked noodles and tofu. Toss gently. Drizzle in the sauce, grind in some pepper, and toss again. Taste to see if you'd like to add more soy sauce or black bean sauce. Serve at once.

Variations

You can use any leafy choy vegetable as a variation of this recipe. Simply trim about an inch off the bottom of the stalk portion, and chop the stems and leaves as directed for the Chinese broccoli. If authentic Asian greens are unavailable, try using 3 baby bok choys, sliced, or a bunch of broccolini, cut into 1-inch sections crosswise, plus 3 to 4 ounces baby spinach or arugula.

Hoisin-Glazed Bok Choy with Tofu & Soba Noodles

4 to 6 servings

Serve this quick, delicious dish of tofu and greens with a hint of citrus on its own or over hot cooked grains—rice, millet, or quinoa. It's also good served over noodles.

1	**8-ounce package soba noodles**
⅓	**cup sliced or slivered almonds**
1	**14- to 16-ounce tub extra-firm tofu**
2	**tablespoons olive or other healthy vegetable oil**
6	**stalks bok choy or 2 baby bok choy, sliced diagonally, leaves chopped**
12	**or so baby carrots, quartered lengthwise, or 3 medium carrots, peeled and sliced diagonally**
2	**scallions, white and green parts, thinly sliced**
2	**teaspoons grated fresh or jarred ginger**
¼	**cup hoisin sauce**
¼	**cup orange juice, preferably fresh**
1	**tablespoon soy sauce or tamari, or to taste**
	Freshly ground pepper to taste

Cook the noodles according to package directions until *al dente,* then drain.

Heat a stir-fry pan or large skillet. Add the almonds and toast on the dry skillet over medium heat, stirring frequently, until very lightly browned. Transfer to a plate and set aside.

Drain the tofu and cut into 6 slabs crosswise. Blot the tofu well between layers of paper towel or a clean kitchen towel, then cut into dice.

Heat the oil in the same pan. Add the tofu and sauté over medium-high heat until it's golden brown on most sides, stirring frequently.

Add the bok choy, carrots, scallions, and ginger. Sauté for a minute or two, until the bok choy leaves wilt a bit, then add the hoisin sauce and orange juice. Turn the heat up to high and cook, stirring, just for a minute or two longer. Remove from the heat.

Add the noodles and toss with the other ingredients in the pan. Season with soy sauce and pepper and serve at once.

SATISFYING VEGGIE COMBOS

Italian Vegetable Ragout with Chard

6 servings

This quick, hearty dish can be served over grains, pasta, or polenta. Although I prefer chard in this delicious ragout, there's no reason not to substitute other greens, such as those suggested as variations, below, or any others you may have on hand.

<table>
<tr><td>2</td><td>tablespoons extra-virgin olive oil</td></tr>
<tr><td>1</td><td>medium onion, finely chopped</td></tr>
<tr><td>3</td><td>to 4 cloves garlic, minced</td></tr>
<tr><td>1</td><td>small eggplant, diced (see note)</td></tr>
<tr><td>1</td><td>to 1½ cups sliced cremini or baby bella mushrooms</td></tr>
<tr><td>1</td><td>medium zucchini, or 1 yellow summer squash</td></tr>
<tr><td>1</td><td>15- to 16-ounce can diced tomatoes (use Italian-style or fire-roasted)</td></tr>
<tr><td>1</td><td>teaspoon dried oregano</td></tr>
<tr><td>½</td><td>teaspoon dried thyme</td></tr>
<tr><td>10</td><td>to 12 ounces chard (any variety)</td></tr>
<tr><td>¼</td><td>cup minced fresh parsley</td></tr>
<tr><td>6</td><td>to 8 leaves fresh basil, thinly sliced</td></tr>
<tr><td>¼</td><td>cup sliced oil-cured sun-dried tomatoes, or more, to taste</td></tr>
<tr><td></td><td>Salt and freshly ground pepper to taste</td></tr>
<tr><td></td><td>Dried hot red pepper flakes to taste</td></tr>
</table>

Heat the oil in a steep-sided stir fry pan or large steep-sided skillet. Add the onion and sauté over medium-low heat until translucent. Add the garlic and continue to sauté until both are golden.

Layer the eggplant, mushrooms, and squash in the pan in that order and pour in ½ cup water. Cover and cook over medium heat for 5 minutes.

Add the tomatoes, oregano, and thyme, and give everything a good stir. Stir in the chard. Cover and continue to simmer over low heat for 5 to 10 minutes, or until the vegetables are just tender.

Meanwhile, strip or cut the chard leaves away from the stems. Slice the stems thinly, and cut the leaves into narrow ribbons.

Stir in the parsley, basil, and dried tomatoes. Season with salt and pepper, and give the dish some subtle heat with the red pepper flakes.

NOTE: You can use any of the very small varieties of eggplant—purple, Japanese, red striped, or white—in this recipe. The skin is tender on these varieties and you don't need to peel them.

Variations

To make the dish more substantial, you can add 2 cups cooked cannellini or chickpeas, or one 15- to 16-ounce can cannellini or chickpeas, drained and rinsed.

This recipe is also good with broccoli rabe, escarole, or any variety of kale or spinach. You can also add beet greens or substitute them for part of the chard.

Greens with Polenta Wedges

4 to 6 servings

Little wedges of precooked polenta add immense charm to this simple vegetable dish. The flavor and texture of polenta is especially compatible with leafy greens.

- 1 **18-ounce tube precooked polenta**
- 2 **tablespoons olive oil**
- 3 **to 4 cloves garlic, minced or thinly sliced**
- 8 **to 10 ounces kale or chard, any variety of either green**
- 4 **to 6 ounces baby spinach**
- 1 **tablespoon balsamic vinegar**
- ¼ **cup sliced oil-cured sun-dried tomatoes, or more, as desired**
  Salt and freshly ground pepper to taste

Cut the polenta into ½ inch thick slices. Cut each slice into 4 little wedges.

Heat a wide nonstick skillet. Add a drop of the oil and spread it around with a paper towel, reserving the rest. Add the polenta wedges; cook them in a single layer over medium heat, about 5 minutes on each side, or until the wedges turn golden and crisp. Put them on a plate and set them aside.

Meanwhile, stem the greens and tear or cut them into large shreds.

In the same skillet, heat the remaining oil. Add the garlic and sauté it over low heat until it just turns golden. Add the kale or chard and a small amount of water (just enough to keep the skillet moist); then cover and steam the mixture for 3 to 5 minutes, or until the greens have wilted down and are bright green and nearly tender.

Add the spinach, cover, and steam for just a minute or two until the leaves have wilted down. Drizzle in the balsamic vinegar and stir quickly to coat the greens.

Gently fold the polenta wedges in with the greens. Stir in the dried tomatoes. Season with salt and pepper and serve at once.

Kale & Cabbage Colcannon

6 servings

In this Irish classic, potatoes and cabbage—or kale—are lightly browned in a skillet. Here I've used both types of greens, and with a generous portion of leeks, it's tastier than ever.

- 6 **medium red-skinned or golden potatoes**
- ½ **cup rice milk**
- 2 **tablespoons olive oil**
- 2 **medium leeks, white and palest green parts only, chopped and well rinsed**
- 2 **cups thinly sliced white cabbage**
- 8 **ounces kale, any variety, stems removed, and thinly sliced**
- ¼ **cup minced fresh parsley**

  Salt and freshly ground pepper to taste

Cook, bake, or microwave the potatoes in their skins until they're easily pierced. When the potatoes are cool enough to handle, peel and cut them into large chunks and place them in a bowl. Mash the potatoes coarsely and stir in the rice milk.

Heat half of the oil in a large skillet. Add the leeks and sauté them over medium heat, covered, for 2 to 3 minutes, or until they're wilted. Add the cabbage and continue to sauté, covered, adding a small amount of water to keep the bottom of the skillet moist, for 2 minutes longer.

Add the kale and remaining oil and sauté, uncovered, until the cabbage begins to turn golden. If the skillet becomes dry, add small amounts of water as needed.

Turn the heat up to medium-high and stir in the potatoes and parsley. Sauté without stirring until the bottom of the mixture gets nicely browned. Stir and allow more of the mixture to brown. Season with salt and pepper, and serve.

Collard Ribbons with Spaghetti Squash

6 servings

If you like spaghetti squash, you'll love how nicely it synergizes with collard ribbons. This recipe has definitely become my favorite way to use spaghetti squash; it's almost as satisfying and comforting as a pasta dish.

1	**small spaghetti squash**
1	**tablespoon olive oil**
1	**large red onion, quartered and thinly sliced**
3	**to 4 cloves garlic, minced**
10	**to 12 ounces collard greens**
½	**teaspoon curry powder**
½	**teaspoon paprika**
⅓	**cup oil-cured sun-dried tomatoes, cut into strips, plus 2 tablespoons of the oil, reserved**
¼	**cup minced fresh parsley, or to taste**
	Salt and freshly ground pepper to taste
	Dried hot red pepper flakes to taste, optional

Preheat the oven to 400°F.

Cut the squash in half lengthwise. Remove the stem and seeds. Then place the squash, cut side up, in a casserole dish with ½ inch of water. Cover the dish tightly with foil and bake the squash for about 40 to 45 minutes until it can easily be pierced with a fork. When the squash is cool enough to handle, scrape it lengthwise with a fork to remove the spaghetti-like strands of flesh.

Heat the oil in a large skillet. Add the onion and sauté over medium heat until translucent. Add the garlic and continue to sauté until the onion is golden.

Cut the collard leaves neatly away from the stems with kitchen shears. Stack 5 or 6 leaves that are roughly the same size, and the roll them up snugly from one of the narrow ends, then slice them thinly. Chop in a few places to shorten the ribbons.

Add the collard greens and a small amount of water to the skillet (just enough to keep it moist); turn up the heat and cook the greens, stirring them frequently, until they're bright green.

Stir in the spaghetti squash strands, curry powder, and paprika. Continue to cook and stir the squash for 5 to 7 minutes longer, or until the collard ribbons are tender, but still nice and bright. Add the dried tomatoes and their oil, and the parsley. Season the mixture with salt, pepper, and the red pepper flakes, if you're using them. Serve at once.

Hoisin-Glazed Collard Greens & Sweet Potatoes

4 to 6 servings

There's something so enticing about the sweet-and-pungent flavor of hoisin sauce enveloping the earthy-sweet flavors of collards and sweet potatoes. Give this recipe a try and see if you love it as much as I do.

- **10 to 14 ounces collard greens**
- **2 tablespoons olive oil**
- **1 medium red onion, quartered and thinly sliced**
- **2 large or 3 medium sweet potatoes**
- **¼ cup hoisin sauce**
- **1 tablespoon reduced-sodium soy sauce**
- **2 tablespoons maple syrup or agave nectar**
- **Dried hot red pepper flakes to taste, optional**

Cut the collard leaves neatly away from the stems with kitchen shears. Stack 5 or 6 leaves that are roughly the same size, and roll them up snugly, starting from one of the narrow ends, then slice them thinly. Chop the slices in a few places to shorten the ribbons. Set them aside.

Heat half of the oil in a large skillet. Add the onion and sauté over medium-low heat until they're golden and tender.

Meanwhile, peel the sweet potatoes. Cut them in half lengthwise, then into ¼-inch-thick half slices. Add them to the skillet along with ½ cup water. Cover and steam the sweet potatoes until they're just tender, but still firm.

Stir in the hoisin sauce, soy sauce, and syrup or agave nectar. Turn the heat up to medium-high and cook the mixture, gently stirring it with a spatula. Add small amounts of water to continually deglaze the skillet, until the sweet potato is tender and nicely glazed. Gently season them with dried hot red pepper flakes, if desired. Cover and set aside.

Heat the remaining oil in another skillet or stir-fry pan. Add the collard greens and a small amount of water (just enough to keep the skillet moist); turn up the heat and cook the greens, stirring frequently, for about 3 to 4 minutes until they're bright green and tender-crisp. Remove the pan from the heat and gently stir the greens into the skillet with the sweet potatoes. Serve at once.

GREENS WITH ROASTED VEGETABLES

Strips of kale or collard greens are a delectable addition to roasted vegetable mixtures. They embellish orange vegetables (squashes, sweet potatoes, carrots) and roots (parsnips, rutabaga, turnips, and the like), as well as roasted veggie combos that feature eggplant or white or golden potatoes. Be sure to stir in fast-cooking strips of cut kale or collards about 5 to 10 minutes before sturdier veggies will finish cooking. That way, all the ingredients will be done at the same time.

Cumin-Roasted Cauliflower & Kale

6 servings

Here's a pretty and easy-to-make medley in which green, white, and red veggies complement each other nicely. You can find cumin seeds just as easily as ground cumin in the spice aisle of a well-stocked supermarket or natural foods store, so give them a try for a subtle burst of flavor.

1   **medium head cauliflower, cut into large bite-size florets**

2   **tablespoons safflower or other high-heat vegetable oil**

1   **medium red bell pepper, cut into narrow strips**

8   **to 12 ounces kale, any variety**

1   **to 2 teaspoons cumin seeds, to taste**

   Salt and freshly ground pepper to taste

Preheat the oven to 425°F.

Combine the cauliflower with the oil in a mixing bowl and toss together. Transfer the mixture to a foil-lined roasting pan and roast for 10 minutes. Stir the cauliflower and add the bell pepper. Roast for 10 minutes longer, or until the vegetables start to brown.

Meanwhile, strip the kale leaves away from the stems and cut them into large, bite-size pieces. Thinly slice the stems, or if you prefer, discard them.

Sprinkle the cumin seeds into the roasting pan and toss them with the vegetables. Pile the kale into the roasting pan, cover it with foil, and roast for 5 to 7 minutes or until the kale is wilted. Stir the kale in with the cauliflower and peppers and continue to roast the mixture briefly, just until everything is lightly roasted but not overdone (the kale shouldn't turn into chips in this recipe).

Transfer to a serving container, season with salt and pepper, and serve.

Garlicky Potatoes with Greens & Olives

4 servings

Lots of garlic and briny olives add spark to the harmonious pairing of potatoes and dark leafy greens.

6 to 7 medium Yukon Gold potatoes, scrubbed

10 to 12 ounces chard or kale (any variety of either), or collard greens

2 tablespoons extra-virgin olive oil

6 cloves garlic, minced

½ cup pitted brine-cured black olives, such as kalamata

1 tablespoon lemon juice, or more, to taste

1 teaspoon dried basil or tarragon

Salt and freshly ground pepper to taste

Microwave the potatoes until just barely tender, starting with 1 minute per potato and adding a small amount of additional time as needed. Or prebake the potatoes, if the oven is already on. Plunge the potatoes into cold water. When they're cool enough to handle, cut them into thick slices.

If you're using chard, cut the leaves away from the stems and chop them coarsely or cut them into ribbons. If you plan to use the stems from chard, trim an inch or so away from the bottoms, then thinly slice the stems. If you're using kale or collard greens, strip the leaves from the stems and cut them into narrow ribbons or small bite-size pieces.

Heat the oil in a wide skillet. Add the garlic and sauté it over low heat for a minute or so, just until it loses its raw quality.

Add the potatoes and greens. Add about ¼ cup water, turn the heat up to medium high, and cook the mixture for about 4 to 5 minutes, stirring frequently, until the potatoes are touched with light brown here and there, and the greens are tender but still nice and green. It's fine if the potatoes break apart.

Remove the mixture from the heat. Stir in the olives, and add lemon juice to taste. Sprinkle in the basil or tarragon, and season with salt (you won't need much) and pepper. Serve at once.

Variation

This recipe works nicely with mustard greens and escarole as well. Chop them coarsely or cut them into ribbons. Add the greens 2 or 3 minutes after you add the potatoes, since you don't want them to cook too long.

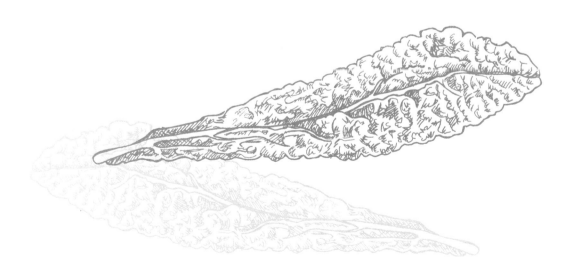

Rosemary Potatoes & Collard Greens with Vegan Sausage

4 to 6 servings

This bountiful skillet makes a quick dinner or a hearty, cold-weather brunch.

- 4 medium-large Yukon Gold or red-skinned potatoes
- 1 large sweet potato
- 10 to 12 ounces collard greens
- 2 tablespoons extra-virgin olive oil
- 3 to 4 cloves garlic, minced
- ¼ cup dry white wine or water
- 2 links Tofurky or Field Roast vegan sausage, cut into ½-inch-thick slices
- Leaves from 2 sprigs fresh rosemary
- 1 teaspoon sweet paprika
- ¼ teaspoon dried hot red pepper flakes, or to taste
- Salt and freshly ground pepper to taste

Cook, bake, or microwave the potatoes and sweet potato until they can be pierced with a fork but are still firm. When they're cool enough to handle, peel and cut the potatoes and sweet potato in half lengthwise, then cut into ½-inch-thick half circles.

Cut the collard greens away from the stems. Stack several leaves at a time, rolling them up snugly from the narrow end. Cut into narrow ribbons.

Heat the oil in a large skillet. Add the garlic and sauté over low heat until golden. Add the collard greens. Turn the heat up to medium-high and cook, stirring frequently, until the collards are bright green and just tender-crisp. Add the potatoes, sausages, and wine or water. Turn the heat down to medium, and sauté the mixture until the potatoes and sausage are touched with golden spots here and there.

Sprinkle in the rosemary, paprika, and red pepper flakes, and sauté for 2 to 3 minutes longer, stirring frequently. Season with salt and pepper, and serve.

Variation

This preparation works well with any variety of kale or chard.

Smoky Potatoes with Turnip Greens

4 to 6 servings

Think of this recipe as a smoky, spicy, Southern U.S.–inflected version of colcannon, the famous Irish potato-and-cabbage dish (see page 129 for Kale & Cabbage Colcannon). It's a great choice for the all-too-rare occasion when you get a nice, large bunch of turnip greens from your CSA or farmers' market.

- 2 **tablespoons olive oil**
- 3 **to 4 shallots, thinly sliced**
- 4 **cloves garlic, minced**
- 6 **medium potatoes, peeled and cut into ½-inch dice**
- 1 **bunch turnip greens (large or small), stemmed and sliced**
- 2 **tablespoons apple cider vinegar**
- 1 **teaspoon sweet paprika**
- 1 **teaspoon smoked paprika, more or less to taste**
- ½ **teaspoon mesquite-flavored seasoning or liquid smoke, more or less to taste**
- ⅓ **cup sliced sun-dried tomatoes (oil-cured or not, as desired)**
-    **Salt and freshly ground pepper or cayenne to taste**

Heat the oil in a steep-sided skillet or stir-fry pan. Add the shallots, and sauté them over low heat until they're translucent. Add the garlic and continue to sauté until both are golden.

Add the potatoes and 1 cup water. Bring to a slow boil, then cover and simmer gently until the potatoes are tender, about 15 minutes. Mash about a quarter of the potatoes, just enough to create a thick base for the dish.

Add the greens, a batch at a time if need be, and cook, covered, for about 5 minutes, until the greens are wilted and just tender.

Add the remaining ingredients, adjusting amounts so that the dish is smoky and spicy to your liking, and cook over low heat for 5 minutes longer. Add a small amount of additional water, if necessary (the consistency should be nice and moist, but not soupy), then serve at once.

Roasted Eggplant Curry with Greens & Tomatoes

4 to 6 servings

This vegetable dish is inspired by a classic Indian dish called *baingan bharta*. The twist here is, not surprisingly, the addition of greens. Once the eggplant has been roasted and is cool enough to handle, this dish comes together quickly.

2   medium eggplants (about 1½ pounds total)

8   to 10 ounces mustard greens, spinach, or chard (any variety)

1   tablespoon olive oil

1   medium onion, finely chopped

1   small fresh hot chili, seeded and minced, or other hot seasoning to taste (see note)

1   14- to 16-ounce can diced tomatoes, with liquid

1   teaspoon good-quality curry powder or garam masala (Indian ground spice mixture)

1   teaspoon ground cumin

½   teaspoon dry mustard

½   teaspoon natural granulated sugar

Salt to taste

Chopped fresh cilantro to taste

Preheat the oven to 425°F.

Prick the skin of the eggplants in several places. Place them on a foil-lined baking sheet and put them in the oven. Bake the eggplants for 35 to 45 minutes, or until they have collapsed. Remove them from the oven and let them cool. When they're cool enough to handle, scoop the flesh away from the skin. Discard the skin and stems and coarsely chop the eggplant flesh.

If you're using mustard greens, trim the stem and chop it coarsely or cut it into ribbons. If you're using any variety of spinach other than baby spinach, trim long stems and chop them coarsely. Use baby spinach leaves whole. If you're using any variety of chard, cut the leaves away from the stems and chop them coarsely or cut them into ribbons. If you plan to use the stems from chard, trim an inch or so away from the bottom, then thinly slice them.

Heat the oil in a large skillet. Add the onion and sauté it over medium heat until it's golden, then add the minced chili and sauté it for another minute or two.

Add the chopped eggplant, tomatoes, spices, and sugar. Stir the mixture well; bring it to a simmer, then cook it over medium-low heat, covered, for 10 minutes.

Add the greens (as well as the stems from chard, if you're using them), a bit at a time, then cover and cook the greens until they're just wilted. Season the greens to taste with salt and remove them from heat. Stir in the chopped cilantro and serve.

NOTE: If you are not inclined to use fresh chilies, simply season the dish to taste with another spicy seasoning like Thai red curry paste or dried hot red pepper flakes.

Variations

To make this a delicious main dish, add 2 cups cooked chickpeas, or one 15- to 16-ounce can chickpeas (drained and rinsed), and serve over quinoa, brown basmati rice, or couscous.

You can use a small amount of chopped beet greens in addition to or in place of the suggested greens.

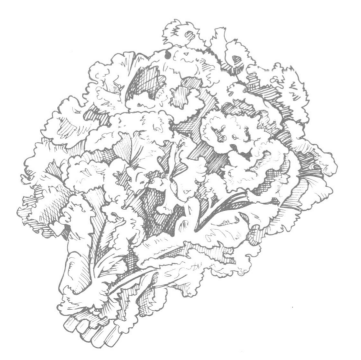

CHAPTER 3

SALADS, DRESSINGS & DIPS

aking salads filled with leafy greens is nothing new. What makes this chapter unique is the large part played by kale. Until recently, most people cooked kale, rather than eating it raw. Credit goes to the raw food movement for popularizing kale as a versatile salad green. And while there's nothing wrong with using lettuce as a base for salads, the entire enterprise becomes that much more intriguing—and nutritious—when you add green leaves like watercress, arugula, and bok choy to the bowl.

MASSAGED KALE SALADS

Kale Salad with Dried Fruits & Nuts, 146

Kale & Red Quinoa Salad, 147

Kale Salad with Fresh Fruit & Radicchio or Red Cabbage, 148

Southwestern-Flavored Kale Salad, 149

Kale Salad with Cauliflower & Sweet Potatoes, 150

Kale & Cucumber Salad with Avocado-Tahini Dressing, 151

Kale Salad with Asian Flavors, 152

Asian-Flavored Kale & Napa Cabbage Slaw, 153

TENDER GREENS SALADS

Spring Greens & Berries Salad, 154

Orange & Cucumber Salad with Spring Greens, 155

Sumptuous Spring Greens Salad, 156

Grated Carrot Salad with Watercress & Parsley, 157

Pinto Bean Salad with Watercress & Dill, 158

Spinach, Watercress & Bok Choy Salad, 159

Three-Potato Salad with Arugula, 160

Spring Greens Salad with Black Beans & Apricots, 161

Roasted Beets & Fennel Salad with Beet Greens & Oranges, 162

Mixed Greens Salad with Mustard Greens, Apples & Pecans, 164

Bok Choy Salad with Red Cabbage & Snow Peas, 166

Tatsoi or Mizuna & Bok Choy Salad, 167

DRESSINGS & DIPS

Sesame-Ginger Salad Dressing, 168

French Dressing, 169

Green Goodness Salad Dressing, 170

Spinach or Arugula & Miso Pesto, 171

Dilled Watercress & Silken Tofu Dip, 172

Very Green Avocado-Tahini Dip, 173

MASSAGED KALE: BASIC TECHNIQUES

Massaged kale salads are a huge trend fueled by the raw food movement, and one well worth promoting. I think the common curly green kale is the best of all the varieties to use in raw salads. To my taste buds it has the mildest, sweetest flavor. I've tried using lacinato and Russian kale in raw salads, and while they're not bad, they don't soften up as nicely as the common curly variety.

I was first introduced to this kind of salad by my friend Harry Lipstein and was amazed by how applying just a bit of muscle to these sturdy greens softens and gives them a wonderfully satisfying crunchy-soft consistency—one that makes a great backdrop for a variety of salads.

We part company on technique, though. Harry prefers the sea-salt method of massaging kale, while I like the "olive oil on the palms" method. A third way is to drizzle oil and lemon juice onto the cut kale before working it in with your hands. All three methods are easy and work well; using one or the other is simply a matter of personal preference.

Whichever method or variety you use, first strip the kale leaves from the stems. If you want to use the stems, slice them very thinly and set them aside. Cut the kale into ribbons or bite-size pieces and give them a good rinse. Before massaging the kale, let the leaves dry, either by spreading them on a clean kitchen towel and letting them air-dry, blotting them between layers of paper towel, or drying them in a salad spinner. The cut kale does not need to be perfectly dry, but you don't want much moisture clinging to the leaves. Transfer them to a large bowl and massage the leaves using one of these three methods:

- Sprinkle ½ to 1 teaspoon of sea salt onto the kale. Massage it into the leaves for 1 to 2 minutes, until they soften and turn bright green.

- Rub a small amount of olive oil onto your palms and massage the kale leaves for 30 to 60 seconds, until they turn bright green and soften.

🖎 Drizzle a small amount of olive oil and lemon juice onto the greens and massage them for 30 to 60 seconds, until they turn bright green and soften.

Once the kale is prepared, there's no limit to the kinds of salads you can create with them. Even if you don't use an entire bunch of kale as the main green in a salad, you can use this technique for just a few leaves and add them to green salads as well as grain or pasta salads. Add some massaged kale to roasted vegetables one they've cooled—roots, eggplant, squashes—and dress with a vinaigrette. Use massaged kale in place of all or some of the lettuce in a Greek-style salad, with kalamata olives, stuffed grape leaves (cut in half) or marinated artichoke hearts, tomatoes, and cucumbers. Or stir very thin slices of massaged kale into your favorite bean salad. Black beans, mango, and kale tossed with a fruity chutney—bliss!

MASSAGED KALE SALADS

Kale Salad with Dried Fruits & Nuts

6 to 8 servings

This basic preparation is beyond delicious—I don't think I've ever served it without being asked for the recipe. It also highlights how appealing raw kale can be.

- 8 to 12 ounces kale, preferably curly green
- ⅔ cup dried fruit of your choice—raisins, cranberries, cherries, chopped apricots, etc.
- ½ cup crushed toasted cashews, pecans, or walnuts
- 2 tablespoons extra-virgin olive oil

  Juice of ½ to 1 lemon, to taste
- 1 tablespoon agave nectar

  Salt and freshly ground pepper to taste

Use one of the three techniques for massaging kale described on pages 144 to 145.

Stir in the remaining ingredients and serve at once.

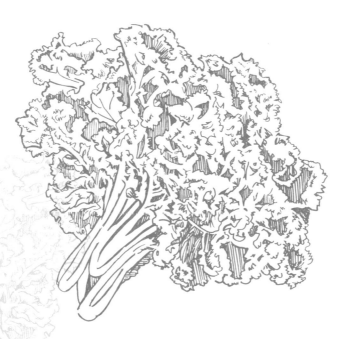

Kale & Red Quinoa Salad

6 or more servings

Think of this salad as a 21st century–style tabouleh. It's packed with nutritious ingredients, yet it's gorgeous and tasty enough to be a crowd-pleasing party or potluck dish.

- 1 **cup red quinoa, rinsed in a fine sieve**
- 8 **to 10 ounces of kale, preferably curly green**
- 2 **tablespoons extra-virgin olive oil**
- 2 **cups cooked fresh or thawed frozen corn kernels**
- 1 **15- to 16-ounce can black beans, drained and rinsed**
- 1 **cup halved grape or cherry tomatoes**
- 2 **tablespoons lemon juice, or more, to taste**
- 1 **teaspoon ground cumin**
- ¼ **cup minced fresh parsley, or more, to taste**
  Salt and freshly ground pepper to taste
- ¼ **cup toasted pumpkin seeds for garnish**

Combine the quinoa with 2 cups water in a medium saucepan. Bring to a rapid simmer, then lower the heat, cover, and simmer gently for about 15 minutes until the stock is absorbed. Allow the cooked quinoa to cool to room temperature.

In a large serving bowl, use one of the three techniques for massaging kale described on pages 144 to 145.

Add cooled quinoa to the serving bowl along with the remaining ingredients. Stir well, sprinkle with pumpkin seeds, and serve.

Kale Salad with Fresh Fruit & Radicchio or Red Cabbage

8 servings

This beautiful, simple salad provides a gorgeous burst of color for everyday or special-occasion meals. It's so sweet and luscious that I consider this to be the salad equivalent of candy.

8 to 10 ounces kale, preferably curly green

1½ cups thinly sliced radicchio or red cabbage

2 medium Bosc pears, quartered lengthwise, cored, and sliced

⅔ cup chopped toasted pecans

Lemon juice to taste

½ cup store-bought fruity salad dressing
(such as raspberry vinaigrette or papaya poppy seed)

Salt and freshly ground pepper to taste

In a large serving bowl, use one of the three techniques for massaging kale described on pages 144 to 145. Add the remaining ingredients, toss together, and serve.

Southwestern-Flavored Kale Salad

6 to 8 servings

Kale, corn, avocado, and tomatoes add up to a seriously delicious salad. If you add beans, it's a hearty main dish; without them, this southwestern-flavored salad is a great companion to tortilla specialties—burritos, enchiladas, and the like—that contain beans.

8   to 10 ounces kale, preferably curly green

2   cups cooked fresh or frozen corn kernels

1   medium firm, ripe avocado, peeled and diced

3   medium tomatoes, diced

1   medium red bell pepper, cut into short, narrow strips

½   cup green pimiento olives

2   cups cooked or drained and rinsed black beans
    or pinto beans, optional

2   to 3 scallions, green parts only, sliced

2   tablespoons extra-virgin olive oil

Juice of 1 lime, more or less to taste

¼   cup minced fresh cilantro, optional

Salt and freshly ground pepper to taste

In a large serving bowl, use one of the three techniques for massaging kale described on pages 144 to 145.

Add the remaining ingredients and toss together gently (use salt sparingly, if at all). Let the salad stand for 10 to 15 minutes, then serve.

Kale Salad with Cauliflower & Sweet Potatoes

6 to 8 servings

Another colorful kale combo, this salad features lightly cooked cauliflower and sweet potatoes, making it fairly substantial as salads go. Though the veggies tend to be sweet and mild in this salad, the extravaganza of textures makes it exciting.

- 1 **medium sweet potato**
- 2 **cups small cauliflower florets**
- 8 **ounces kale, preferably curly green**
- 1 **medium firm ripe avocado, diced**
- 1 **medium red bell pepper, cut into narrow 2-inch strips**
- 2 **scallions, thinly sliced**
- ¼ **cup minced fresh parsley**
- 2 **tablespoons extra-virgin olive oil**
- 2 **tablespoons red wine vinegar**
- **Juice of ½ to 1 lime, to taste**
- 1 **tablespoon agave nectar**
- ½ **teaspoon dried tarragon**
- ¼ **teaspoon dried thyme**
- **Salt and freshly ground pepper to taste**

Microwave or bake the sweet potato ahead of time; cook until done but still nice and firm. When cool, peel and cut into ½-inch dice.

Steam the cauliflower until just tender-crisp and refresh immediately under cold water to stop the steaming. Allow the cauliflower to drain for a few minutes in a colander. If you like cauliflower raw, skip this step.

In a large serving bowl, use one of the three techniques for massaging kale described on pages 144 to 145.

Add the remaining ingredients and toss together gently and thoroughly. Let the salad stand for 20 to 30 minutes at room temperature, then serve.

Kale & Cucumber Salad
with Avocado-Tahini Dressing

6 servings

Massaged kale served simply with cucumbers, carrots, and a luscious dressing of avocado and tahini is an incredible treat.

8 **to 10 ounces kale, preferably curly green**

1 **medium cucumber, quartered lengthwise, seeds cut away, and sliced**

1 **cup grated carrot**

¼ **to ½ cup minced fresh parsley**

2 **scallions, green parts only, thinly sliced**

Avocado-Tahini Dressing (page 66), as desired

Salt and freshly ground pepper to taste

In a large serving bowl, use one of the three techniques for massaging kale described on pages 144 to 145.

Combine the kale with the remaining ingredients in a serving bowl. Toss together and serve.

Kale Salad with Asian Flavors

6 to 8 servings

As a salad green, kale is quite compatible with Asian flavors. I especially like this salad with napa cabbage, but green and savoy cabbages work just as well.

 8 to 10 ounces kale, preferably curly green
 2 cups thinly shredded napa, green, or savoy cabbage
12 or so baby carrots, quartered lengthwise
 1 15-ounce can baby corn, drained
 3 stalks bok choy with leaves, sliced, or 1 baby bok choy, sliced
    Sesame-Ginger Salad Dressing (page 168), as desired
 ¼ cup or so crushed peanuts or cashews, optional
    Freshly ground pepper to taste

In a large serving bowl, use one of the three techniques for massaging kale described on pages 144 to 145.

Combine the kale with the remaining ingredients in a serving bowl. Toss together and serve.

Asian-Flavored Kale & Napa Cabbage Slaw

6 to 8 servings

This salad was inspired by Barbara Pollak, a longtime reader of my books. She forewarned me that it's addictive, and she's right.

FOR THE DRESSING:

- 1 tablespoon olive oil or other healthy vegetable oil
- 1 tablespoon dark sesame oil
- 2 tablespoons vinegar (apple cider, rice, or white wine)
- 2 tablespoon reduced-sodium soy sauce or tamari
- 2 tablespoons agave nectar or other liquid sweetener

- 5 or 6 leaves kale, preferably lacinato (curly kale will work too)
- 3 cups firmly packed thinly shredded napa cabbage
- 1 cup grated carrots
- 1 cup sprouts, any variety
- ¼ cup toasted pumpkin or sunflower seeds, or ⅛ cup of each
- 3 tablespoons sesame seeds
- Freshly ground pepper to taste

Combine the dressing ingredients in a small bowl and whisk together.

Strip the kale leaves from the stems. Slice the stems very thinly or discard. Cut the kale leaves into very thin strips and place in a large serving bowl. Oil your hands lightly and massage the kale for 30 to 45 seconds, until the leaves are bright green and soft.

Add the remaining salad ingredients, then toss well with the dressing. Let the salad stand for 15 minutes. Taste and adjust the tang, saltiness, and sweetness with more vinegar, soy sauce, or sweetener to your liking, then serve.

Spring Greens & Berries Salad

6 servings

This beautiful salad expands upon the classic combination of spinach and strawberries in a salad.

FOR THE FRESH BERRY DRESSING:

½ cup hulled strawberries

2 tablespoons lemon juice

1 tablespoon extra-virgin olive oil

6 ounces or so tender greens (use a combination of baby spinach, arugula, dandelion greens, watercress, and baby bok choy)

1 cup strawberries, hulled and sliced

½ cup fresh blueberries or raspberries

⅓ cup chopped and lightly toasted walnuts or pecans, or 2 to 3 tablespoons toasted pine nuts

Combine the strawberries, lemon juice, and oil in a food processor and pulse until the strawberries are pureed.

Combine the greens, strawberries, and blueberries or raspberries in a serving bowl and toss together.

Pour the dressing on the salad and toss together. Scatter the nuts over the top of the salad and serve.

Orange & Cucumber Salad with Spring Greens

4 to 6 servings

Early-spring greens cross paths with winter citrus in this easy and delectable salad.

½ **English (hothouse) cucumber, thinly sliced**

3 **to 4 small oranges (such as clementines), peeled and sectioned**

2 **big handfuls baby arugula leaves**

1 **baby bok choy, thinly sliced**

½ **bunch watercress leaves**

1 **cup green sprouts (such as pea shoots)**

Toasted pumpkin seeds (pepitas) or sunflower seeds, as desired

Juice of ½ orange

Juice of ½ lemon

1 **teaspoon each lemon and orange zest, or more to taste, optional (but highly recommended)**

1 **to 2 tablespoons extra-virgin olive oil**

Salt and freshly ground pepper to taste

Combine all the ingredients in a serving bowl. Toss together and serve.

Sumptuous Spring Greens Salad

6 or more servings

A nice selection of fresh spring produce needs little embellishment to offer a heaping portion of refreshment.

- 2 **to 3 medium beets, red or golden**
- ½ **bunch watercress leaves,
  or a small bunch chopped young dandelion greens**
- ½ **head radicchio, thinly sliced**
- 1 **Granny Smith apple, quartered, cored, and thinly sliced**
- ½ **medium cucumber, halved lengthwise and thinly sliced**
- 4 **to 6 radishes, or 2 turnips, thinly sliced,
  with their carefully washed and thinly sliced greens**
- 1 **medium ripe avocado, peeled and diced**
- 2 **tablespoons extra-virgin olive oil, or toasted nut oil, more or less
  as desired**
- 2 **tablespoons lemon juice, or more, to taste**

  Salt and freshly ground pepper to taste

Cook or microwave the beets until done but still nice and firm. When the beets are cool enough to handle, peel and dice them.

Combine the beets with all the remaining ingredients in a serving bowl and toss together. Serve at once.

Grated Carrot Salad with Watercress & Parsley

6 servings

This enticing little grated salad is packed with vitamins A and C from the carrots, watercress, and parsley. The sweet carrots and spicy watercress contrast nicely, and the remaining ingredients emphasize their synergy.

- 1 **pound baby carrots**
- 1 **bunch watercress leaves**
- ½ **cup parsley leaves**
- ¼ **cup oil-packed sun-dried tomatoes**
- ¼ **cup walnuts**
- 2 **to 3 tablespoons lemon juice, or to taste**
- 1 **to 2 tablespoons agave nectar, to taste**
- 1 **tablespoon oil from sun-dried tomatoes**
- **Salt and freshly ground pepper to taste**

Grate the carrots in a food processor fitted with a grating blade. Transfer the carrots to a serving bowl.

Combine the watercress, parsley, dried tomatoes, and walnuts in a food processor fitted with a metal blade. Pulse on and off until finely chopped. Don't overprocess!

Transfer the watercress mixture to the serving bowl. Toss together with the carrots. Add the remaining ingredients and stir until well combined. Let the salad stand for 20 to 30 minutes to let the flavors marry, then serve.

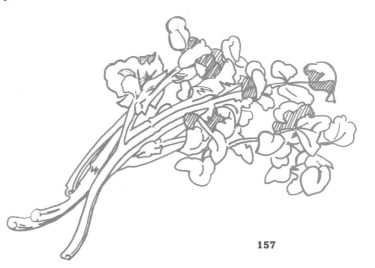

Pinto Bean Salad with Watercress & Dill

6 servings

Here's a simple salad that features the delightful peppery tastes of watercress and dill. This savory salad is also packed with vitamin C.

FOR THE DRESSING:

¼ vegan mayonnaise

1 tablespoon lemon or lime juice, or more, to taste

1 teaspoon prepared mustard

½ teaspoon ground cumin

Salt and freshly ground pepper to taste

1 15- to 16-ounce can pinto beans, drained and rinsed

1 bunch watercress leaves

2 handfuls young arugula or dandelion leaves

2 medium firm, ripe tomatoes, finely diced

¼ cup chopped parsley or cilantro leaves

½ cup sliced kalamata olives

1 medium celery stalk, finely diced

¼ cup chopped fresh dill

In a small bowl, combine the dressing ingredients and mix thoroughly.

Combine the salad ingredients in a serving bowl. Pour the dressing over the salad and toss to combine thoroughly. Season to taste with salt and pepper and serve.

Spinach, Watercress & Bok Choy Salad

8 to 10 servings

Here's a simple salad that features lots of watercress, which is rich in vitamin C. The crunch of baby bok choy contrasts with the tender greens, and French dressing tempers the peppery flavor of the watercress.

2 **to 3 ounces baby spinach leaves**

1 **bunch watercress leaves**

2 **baby bok choy, sliced**

2 **to 3 scallions, thinly sliced**

1 **large celery stalk, finely diced**

1 **cup cherry or grape tomatoes, halved or, if small, left whole**

French Dressing (page 169), as needed

Toasted sunflower seeds for topping, optional

Combine all the ingredients except the dressing in a serving bowl and toss together.

Add enough dressing to lightly coat and toss again; or pass the dressing around separately so that everyone can dress their own salad. If desired, pass around sunflower seeds for topping individual servings.

Variation
Use baby or young arugula, dandelion greens, tatsoi, or mizuna in place of all, or part of, the spinach.

Three-Potato Salad with Arugula

8 servings

This potato salad combines three kinds of potatoes with arugula for an earthy flavor with plenty of eye appeal.

 1 medium sweet potato

 3 medium blue or purple potatoes

 2 medium yellow potatoes

 2 celery stalks, thinly sliced on the diagonal

 ½ medium red bell pepper, finely diced

 ⅓ cup pitted kalamata olives or sun-dried tomatoes, sliced

 2 tablespoons extra-virgin olive oil

 2 to 3 tablespoons apple cider vinegar

 2 to 3 tablespoons minced fresh dill

 Salt and freshly ground pepper to taste

 3 big handfuls arugula leaves, rinsed, stemmed, and chopped,
 or baby arugula leaves, rinsed

 Toasted pumpkin seeds (pepitas)
 or sunflower seeds for topping, as desired

Cook, bake, or microwave the three kinds of potatoes until done but still nice and firm. Plunge into cold water. Let stand until cool enough to handle, then peel and cut into ½- to ¾-inch dice.

Combine the potatoes in a mixing bowl with the celery, bell pepper, olives, olive oil, vinegar, dill, salt, and pepper. Stir together gently.

Stir half of the arugula in with the potatoes and line a serving platter with the rest. Mound the potato salad onto the platter, and scatter the seeds over the top. Serve at once.

Spring Greens Salad with Black Beans & Apricots

4 to 6 servings

Late spring brings beautiful fresh apricots to the market, and these, along with black beans, dress up a salad of peppery greens and other seasonal flavors.

- 4 **fresh apricots**
- 3 **to 4 ounces baby arugula, spinach, tatsoi, or mizuna (or, preferably, a combination)**
- 1 **15- to 16-ounce can black beans, drained and rinsed**

  A good handful of sprouts (pea shoots, broccoli sprouts)
- 3 **to 4 radishes, thinly sliced**

  Handful of radish greens, chopped

  Juice of ½ lemon
- ¼ **cup raspberry vinaigrette**

  Salt and freshly ground pepper to taste
- 2 **to 3 tablespoons toasted pumpkin or sunflower seeds for topping**

Cut the apricots in half lengthwise and remove the pits. Cut each half into quarters lengthwise.

Combine the apricots with all the remaining ingredients except the seeds in a serving bowl and toss together. Sprinkle the seeds over the top and serve.

Roasted Beets & Fennel Salad
with Beet Greens & Oranges

6 to 8 servings

Roasted beets are a delicious addition to salads. Try to incorporate beet greens whenever possible, since they add flavor, nutrition, and visual appeal to the mix.

4 to 5 good-size beets with a good quantity of greens

1 medium fennel bulb, stemmed, trimmed of stalks, and thinly sliced

½ medium red onion, thinly sliced

2 to 3 cloves garlic, sliced

2 tablespoons extra-virgin olive oil or fragrant nut oil

3 small seedless oranges, such as clementines, sectioned

2 tablespoons minced fresh dill

Juice of 1 lemon, or more, to taste

2 teaspoons agave nectar, or more, to taste

Salt and freshly ground pepper to taste

Preheat the oven to 425°F.

Cut the greens away from the beets. Chop coarsely, rinse well, and set aside.

To minimize the mess of cutting raw beets, peel them over the trash or compost container, and slice them on a cutting board covered with wax paper. Place the sliced raw beets in a foil-lined baking dish and combine with the fennel, onion, and garlic. Drizzle with enough oil to coat, reserving the rest.

Bake the beets, stirring them once or twice, for 30 minutes, or until tender to your liking, and touched with brown spots.

Meanwhile, place the beet greens in a medium skillet; steam until bright green and just tender. Place greens in a colander and squeeze out as much liquid as possible. Chop fairly fine.

Combine the roasted vegetables in a mixing bowl with the remaining oil as well as all the remaining ingredients and toss together. Serve warm or at room temperature.

Mixed Greens Salad with Mustard Greens, Apples & Pecans

6 servings

Raw mustard greens alone could be very intense in a salad, but their peppery bite is quite appealing in combination with other greens, sweet apples, and carrots.

- 2   **medium carrots, sliced**
- 2   **medium crisp, sweet apples, cored and diced**
- ½   **medium red onion, thinly sliced, optional**
- 4   **to 6 mustard greens, very thinly shredded**
- 3   **to 4 ounces mixed baby greens**
- ½   **cup toasted pecans**
      French Dressing (page 169), as needed

Combine the ingredients in a serving bowl. Pour enough dressing over the salad to moisten it. Toss together well and serve at once.

Variation

Replace one of the apples with a firm, ripe pear, cored and diced.

RAW TURNIPS OR RADISHES
& THEIR GREENS IN SALADS

Follow the tips in Preparing Turnips or Radishes & Their Greens on page 56. Slice radishes and combine them with their greens in a bowl, drizzle in some olive oil and apple cider vinegar or wine vinegar, and salt and pepper. Or toss the radishes and their greens into any sort of salad.

Raw turnip greens are quite intense and can be bitter when they get larger and older. If you would like to eat these greens raw, stem and slice them very thin, then use one of the techniques for massaging raw kale described on page 144, which will soften and mellow them somewhat.

Combine a small amount of thinly sliced, massaged turnip leaves with grated or diced turnip in a serving bowl (add some grated carrot, too, if you'd like), then dress to taste with apple cider vinegar, white wine vinegar, or rice vinegar; a bit of sugar or a splash of agave nectar; and salt and pepper. Sprinkle with toasted pumpkin or sunflower seeds or some thinly sliced scallions. You can also use a few massaged turnip leaves in a tossed salad with other greens and raw veggies.

Bok Choy Salad with Red Cabbage & Snow Peas

4 to 6 servings

I've been making variations of this salad for many years, and I'm glad to be sharing it here. The combination of crisp snow peas, bok choy, and red cabbage with the salty-tangy flavors of Sesame-Ginger Salad Dressing is most appealing.

- 2 **cups or so snow peas, trimmed**
- 1 **cup mung bean sprouts or other sprouts**
- 5 **to 6 stalks regular bok choy, with leaves, or 2 medium whole baby bok choy, sliced**
- 2 **cups thinly sliced red cabbage**
- 1 **medium red bell pepper, cut into strips**
- 2 **scallions, thinly sliced**
- ¼ **cup minced fresh cilantro, optional**

  Sesame-Ginger Salad Dressing (page 166), as needed

  Freshly ground pepper to taste

  Chopped peanuts or cashews, optional

Combine the snow peas in a small skillet with a small amount of water. If using mung bean sprouts, add those as well (other kinds of sprouts can be left raw). Steam over medium heat for a minute or less, just until the snow peas are bright green and have lost their raw quality. Transfer to a colander and rinse with cool water. Drain well.

Combine the snow peas and sprouts with the bok choy, cabbage, bell pepper, scallions, and cilantro (if you are using it), and toss together. Add enough dressing to moisten, season with pepper, and toss again. Serve at once, passing around chopped peanuts or cashews if desired.

Tatsoi or Mizuna & Bok Choy Salad

4 to 6 servings

This salad makes a lively accompaniment to many types of Asian-style dishes. However, there's no reason to serve it only with Asian-themed meals. It's a simple, offbeat accompaniment to many types of dishes.

    5   to 6 ounces tatsoi or mizuna
    1   cup daikon radish, peeled and cut into thin, half-circle slices
    4   to 6 stalks bok choy, with greens, thinly sliced
    1   cup green sprouts, such as pea shoots
    3   small seedless oranges, such as clementines, sectioned
    2   tablespoons sesame seeds or ¼ cup toasted slivered almonds
        Sesame-Ginger Salad Dressing (page 166), as needed to moisten

Combine the ingredients in a serving bowl and toss together. Serve at once.

Variation
Substitute baby spinach or arugula for the tatsoi or mizuna, or use a combination of greens. If daikon is unavailable, use crisp turnip or jicama.

SALAD DRESSINGS & DIPS

Sesame-Ginger Salad Dressing

About 1 cup

Salty, and just slightly sweet and tangy, this is the perfect dressing for Asian-style salads that feature bok choy and other greens.

- ⅓ **cup olive oil or other healthy vegetable oil**
- 2 **tablespoons dark sesame oil**
- ⅓ **cup rice vinegar or white wine vinegar**
- 1 **tablespoon agave nectar or other liquid sweetener**
- 2 **tablespoons reduced-sodium soy sauce or tamari**
- 2 **teaspoons grated fresh ginger or jarred ginger**
- 1 **tablespoon sesame seeds**

Combine all ingredients in a tightly lidded jar. Shake well before each use.

French Dressing

About 1 cup

Because of the subtle touch of sweetness in this dressing, it's an absolutely fantastic counterpoint to salads that include slightly bitter or sharp greens.

⅓ cup good-quality ketchup

¼ cup olive oil

2 tablespoons red wine vinegar

2 tablespoons vegan mayonnaise

2 teaspoons agave nectar or maple syrup

1 teaspoon paprika

Combine all the ingredients in a small mixing bowl and whisk together until smoothly combined.

Transfer to a covered container or cruet. Use at once, or refrigerate until needed. Bring to room temperature before using. This dressing keeps well in the refrigerator for about a week.

Green Goodness Salad Dressing

About 1½ cups

Greens—the stars of this recipe—make a delicious dressing for grain or bean salads. It's also tasty drizzled on lightly cooked or roasted vegetables.

- ½ **cup extra-virgin olive oil**
- ½ **cup peeled, seeded, and chopped cucumber**
- ½ **cup firmly packed fresh parsley**
- 2 **good handfuls of baby spinach leaves**
- 2 **tablespoons lemon juice**
- 2 **tablespoons white or red wine vinegar**
- 1 **tablespoon chopped fresh dill, or 1 teaspoon dried dill**
- **Freshly ground pepper to taste**

Place all ingredients in the container of a food processor. Process until all that remains of the parsley is tiny flakes. Refrigerate the unused portion in an airtight container. Use within two days.

Spinach or Arugula & Miso Pesto

About 1½ cups, enough for 6 servings

The twist on this classic pesto recipe is the substitution of spinach or arugula for the customary basil, which, though delicious, turns brown quickly. Miso, a salty paste of fermented soybeans (available at any natural food grocery), makes a good nondairy stand-in for Parmesan cheese.

10 to 12 ounces spinach or arugula (regular or baby varieties), well rinsed

½ cup firmly packed fresh parsley leaves

¼ cup pine nuts or walnuts

2 tablespoons extra-virgin olive oil

1 to 2 tablespoons lemon juice, to taste

2 tablespoons white miso, more or less to taste

Freshly ground pepper to taste

Steam the greens until just wilted. When cool enough to handle, squeeze out as much moisture as possible.

Combine greens with the remaining ingredients in the container of a food processor. Process until the mixture is coarsely pureed. Use at once as suggested above; refrigerate any leftovers in an airtight container, where they'll keep for 2 to 3 days.

Dilled Watercress & Silken Tofu Dip

About 1½ cups

This creamy dip benefits from the peppery flavor of watercress. It is delicious served with baby carrots, spoon-size pieces of bell pepper, celery, and other crisp veggies, as well as whole-grain crackers and crispbreads.

1 **12.3-ounce package firm silken tofu**

½ **bunch watercress leaves**

Juice of ½ lemon

1 **scallion, minced**

1 **tablespoon prepared horseradish, optional (but highly recommended)**

2 **tablespoons minced fresh dill, or 1 teaspoon dried dill**

2 **teaspoons all-purpose seasoning blend (such as Spike or Mrs. Dash)**

Salt and freshly ground pepper to taste

Place the tofu in a food processor and process until pureed. Add the watercress leaves, in batches if needed, and pulse on and off until finely chopped.

Add the remaining ingredients, and pulse on and off just until the ingredients are well integrated into the tofu. Transfer to a small serving bowl and serve with any of the suggested accompaniments above.

Very Green Avocado-Tahini Dip

About 1½ cups

A marriage of guacamole and hummus—and infused with a good amount of leafy greens—this rich dip makes its own unique statement. Serve it with tortilla chips, fresh pita, pita chips, raw veggies, or any combination that suits you.

3   **to 4 ounces baby spinach or arugula, or a combination**

1   **large, ripe avocado, peeled and diced**

⅓   **cup tahini (sesame paste)**

     Juice of 1 lemon

½   **teaspoon ground cumin**

2   **tablespoons minced fresh parsley, cilantro, or dill**

     Salt and freshly ground pepper to taste

Rinse the greens and place them in a large skillet or saucepan. With just the water clinging to the leaves, cook the greens until just wilted down. Remove from the heat.

Place all the ingredients in the container of a food processor, and process until smooth. Add ¼ cup water, as needed, to achieve a medium-thick consistency. Transfer to a serving bowl. Keep covered until ready to serve.

Serve at once as suggested above. Store any leftovers in an airtight container in the refrigerator for up to two days.

CHAPTER 4

GREENS IN SOUPS & STEWS

**W**hen it comes to using greens in soups and stews, there's not much to the process other than to clean and cut the greens and stir them into the soup pot at the appropriate time. Still, a wide array of greens is showcased in these preparations, from the tender leafy greens of spring, to hardier chards and kale, to quick-cooking Asian greens. So set a soup or stew pot on the stove, pull out a ladle, and get ready to add green goodness to your table.

SOUPS & STEWS

Hearty Italian-Flavored Chard & Vegetable Soup

6 to 8 servings

You can vary the vegetables and greens in this versatile recipe according to season, availability, and mood. Some excellent variations are suggested below.

2   **tablespoons extra-virgin olive oil**

1   **medium onion, finely chopped**

2   **cloves garlic, minced**

2   **large carrots, diced**

2   **medium potatoes, diced**

2   **large stalks celery, diced**

2   **cups peeled and diced eggplant**

1   **32-ounce container vegetable broth, or 4 cups water with 2 vegetable bouillon cubes**

1   **14- to 16-ounce can diced tomatoes**

1   **14- to 16-ounce can pureed tomatoes**

¼   **cup thinly sliced sun-dried tomatoes (oil-cured or not, as preferred), or more to taste**

1   **teaspoon paprika**

1   **small zucchini, quartered lengthwise and thinly sliced**

8   **to 10 ounces chard, any variety, leaves chopped (use the stems, thinly sliced, if desired)**

¼   **cup minced fresh parsley, or more, to taste**

     Sliced basil leaves to taste

     Salt and freshly ground pepper to taste

Heat the oil in a large soup pot. Add the onion and garlic, and sauté over medium-low heat until golden.

Add the carrots, potatoes, celery, eggplant, and broth. Bring to a simmer, then stir in the diced, pureed, dried tomatoes, and paprika. Return to a simmer, then cover and simmer gently for about 25 minutes until the vegetables are nearly tender.

Add the zucchini and chard and simmer gently, about 8 to 10 minutes longer, until all the vegetables are tender but not overdone.

Stir in the parsley and basil; adjust the consistency with more water if necessary. Season with salt and pepper. Let the soup stand off the heat for an hour or two if time allows, then heat through, or serve at once. If desired, pass around extra chopped basil and/or parsley for topping individual servings.

Variations

This soup is also good with an equivalent amount of kale or escarole. Add it at the same time as you would add the chard. If you have a bunch of beet greens on hand, these would also work in addition to, or in place of, some of the chard.

Italian-Style Potato & Escarole Soup

6 servings

An Italian café in New York City's Chelsea gallery district was serving a soup like this one on a blustery winter day as my husband and I were enjoying the gallery scene. Alas, it had a meat stock, so I was unable to try it. The combination of potatoes, escarole, and chickpeas sounded so good that I made a note of it and decided to create my own version of this comforting soup, which is indeed perfect for a chilly day.

2   tablespoons extra-virgin olive oil

1   medium onion, quartered and thinly sliced

2   to 3 cloves garlic, minced

6   medium or 4 large potatoes, preferably russet or golden, peeled and diced

2   medium carrots, thinly sliced

1   32-ounce carton low-sodium vegetable broth

1   teaspoon dried basil

½   teaspoon dried thyme

1   15- to 16-ounce can chickpeas or cannellini (white beans), drained and rinsed

1   medium head (6 to 8 ounces) escarole, coarsely chopped and rinsed

½   cup chopped fresh parsley

Salt and freshly ground pepper to taste

Heat the oil in a soup pot. Add the onion and sauté over medium heat until translucent. Add the garlic and continue to sauté until both are golden, stirring frequently.

Add the potatoes, carrots, broth, basil, thyme, and 2 cups water. Bring to a gentle boil, then cover and simmer gently for 20 minutes, or until the potatoes and carrots are tender.

Stir in the chickpeas or cannellini, escarole, and half of the parsley. Simmer gently for 8 to 10 minutes, or until the escarole is tender.

With the back of a wooden spoon or a potato masher, mash some of the potatoes right in the soup pot, to give it a nice base. Stir in water as needed (up to 2 cups). The soup should be thick, but not overly so. Return to a simmer. Stir in the remaining parsley, season with salt and pepper, then serve.

If time allows, let the soup stand off the heat for an hour or more before serving, then heat through, as needed.

Variations

This soup is delicious with kale, chard, or broccoli rabe. Use equivalent amounts (as listed in the ingredients list); stem and chop the kale and chard; cut broccoli rabe into ½-inch segments.

Lentil Soup with Greens & Tiny Pasta

8 servings

This is the kind of soup that sticks to your ribs on cold, blustery days; a good bunch of greens augment the hearty duo of lentils and pasta.

- 2   **tablespoons extra-virgin olive oil**
- 1   **large onion, finely chopped**
- 2   **to 3 cloves garlic, minced**
- 2   **medium carrots, thinly sliced**
- 2   **large celery stalks, diced**
- 1   **cup dried lentils, sorted and rinsed**
- 2   **bay leaves**
- 1   **teaspoon paprika**
- ½   **teaspoon each: dried oregano, basil, and thyme**
- 1   **8- to 12-ounce bunch chard or kale, any variety, stemmed and cut into bite-size pieces or ribbons (stems can be thinly sliced and used as well, if desired)**
- 1   **15- to 16-ounce can fire-roasted or Italian-style diced tomatoes**
- ¼   **cup dry red wine, optional**
- ⅔   **cup tiny pasta (such as ditalini, tubetti, or tiny shells)**
- ¼   **cup minced fresh parsley or dill**
-     **Salt and freshly ground pepper to taste**

Heat the oil in a soup pot. Add the onion and garlic and sauté over medium-low heat until the onion is golden.

Add the carrots, celery, lentils, bay leaves, seasonings, and 6 cups water. Bring to a simmer, then cover and simmer gently for 25 to 30 minutes, or until the lentils and vegetables are tender.

Add the greens, tomatoes, and wine (if you are using it), and simmer over low heat for 10 minutes longer, or until the greens are tender to your liking.

Meanwhile, cook the pasta separately in a large saucepan with plenty of rapidly simmering water until *al dente,* then drain. Stir the pasta into the soup, then add the parsley or dill.

Adjust the consistency with a bit more water if it is too thick, then season with salt and pepper, and serve. The soup thickens as it stands; add water and adjust seasonings as needed.

Variation

As with Hearty Italian-Flavored Chard & Vegetable Soup on page 176, beet greens can augment or replace some of the chard here as well.

Sweet Potato & Corn Stew with Hardy Greens

6 to 8 servings

Even though the ingredients for this stew are now available year-round, it is perfect for early fall, when the last of the local corn intersects with the first craving for sweet potatoes. I especially like to prepare it with collard greens, but any variety of kale or chard is just as good.

- 2 tablespoons olive oil
- 1 medium-large red onion, chopped
- 2 cloves garlic, minced
- 2 large or 3 medium sweet potatoes, peeled and diced
- 1 32-ounce carton vegetable broth
- 10 to 12 ounces collard greens, kale, or chard, stemmed and cut into bite-size pieces or ribbons (thinly sliced stems of kale or chard can be used as well, if desired)
- 2 cups fresh corn kernels (from 3 medium ears)
- 2 cups diced ripe tomatoes
- 1 teaspoon ground cumin, or more, to taste
- ¼ to ½ cup minced fresh cilantro or parsley, to taste

  Dried hot red pepper flakes to taste

  Salt and freshly ground pepper to taste

Heat the oil in a soup pot. Add the onion and sauté over medium-low heat until translucent. Add the garlic and continue to sauté until both are golden.

Add the sweet potatoes and broth. Bring to a gentle boil, then lower the heat, cover, and simmer gently for 10 to 15 minutes, or until the sweet potatoes are nearly tender.

Stir in the greens, corn, tomatoes, and cumin. Continue to simmer until the greens and corn are just tender, about 10 minutes. In the soup pot, mash some of the sweet potato with the back of a wooden spoon to thicken the base.

Stir in the cilantro and add just enough red pepper flakes to give the stew a subtle heat. Season with salt and pepper. Serve at once, or if time allows, let the stew stand off the heat for an hour or two. Heat through before serving.

Winter Squash & Red Bean Stew
with Hardy Greens

8 servings

Collards, kale, and chard are all quite compatible with winter squash. This stew, which you can spice boldly or gently, as you prefer, is satisfying and sustaining cold-weather fare.

- 1 tablespoon olive oil
- 1 large onion, chopped
- 3 to 4 cloves garlic, minced
- 1 medium red bell pepper, diced
- 4 heaping cups prebaked, peeled, and diced orange squash (sugar pumpkin, butternut, carnival, etc.)
- 1 28-ounce can diced tomatoes, with liquid
- 2 cups cooked or one 16-ounce can red or black beans, drained and rinsed
- 1 to 2 fresh hot green chili peppers, seeded and minced, or dried hot red pepper flakes, to taste
- 2 teaspoons ground cumin
- 10 to 12 ounces collard greens, kale, or chard, stemmed and cut into bite-size pieces or ribbons (thinly sliced stems of kale or chard can be used)

  Salt and freshly ground pepper to taste
- ¼ cup chopped fresh cilantro

  Hot cooked rice, optional

Heat the oil in a soup pot. Add the onion and sauté over medium heat until translucent. Add the garlic and red bell pepper and continue to sauté until the onion is golden.

Add the squash, tomatoes, beans, chili peppers or pepper flakes, cumin, and 3 cups water. Bring to a gentle boil, then simmer gently, covered, for 10 minutes.

Stir in the greens in batches, until they're all in and wilted, then simmer gently for 10 minutes longer, or until tender to your liking.

Season with salt and pepper, then stir in the cilantro. Serve at once in shallow bowls over hot cooked rice, if desired.

Coconut Cauliflower Curry
with Mustard Greens & Spinach

4 to 6 servings

In this curry, pungent mustard greens are paired with mild spinach, resulting in a gorgeous and satisfying stew. Mustard greens, which are often used in curries (as is spinach) most often come in large bunches. Use as much as you'd like; the sharp flavor is well tempered by cooking.

1½ **tablespoons olive oil**

1 **large onion, quartered and thinly sliced**

2 **to 3 cloves garlic, minced**

3 **medium-large potatoes, peeled and diced**

3 **medium carrots, sliced**

1 **15-ounce can light coconut milk**

½ **medium head cauliflower, cut into bite-size pieces**

1 **small fresh hot chili, seeded and minced, optional**

1 **to 2 teaspoons grated fresh ginger, to taste**

2 **to 3 teaspoons good-quality curry powder, or to taste**

½ **teaspoon turmeric**

½ **to 1 bunch mustard greens
(depending on size and how much you like them),
cut into bite-size pieces or ribbons**

4 **to 6 ounces spinach, any variety, stemmed and chopped,
or equivalent amount of baby spinach, left whole**

Salt and freshly ground pepper to taste

Heat the oil in a large soup pot. Add the onion and sauté over medium heat until translucent. Add the garlic and continue to sauté until the onion is golden.

Add the potatoes, carrots, and 2 cups water, and bring to a simmer. Cover and simmer gently for 10 to 15 minutes, or until the potatoes are about half tender.

Add the coconut milk, cauliflower, chili (if you are using it), ginger, curry powder, and turmeric. Cover and continue to simmer gently for 10 minutes, then stir in the mustard greens. Cover and simmer for 10 minutes longer, or until greens and other vegetables are tender but still retain their colors.

Mash some of the potatoes against the side of the pot with a wooden spoon to thicken the base. Add the spinach and cover; let it wilt down, stir it in, then season with salt and pepper. Serve at once.

Puree of Green Peas & Spring Greens

6 to 8 servings

This ultra-green soup is a wonderful way to welcome spring and an excellent way to utilize early-spring greens.

- 2 tablespoons light olive oil
- 2 large or 3 medium leeks,
  white and palest green parts only, chopped
- 2 to 3 cloves garlic, minced
- 1 32-ounce carton vegetable broth
- 1 16-ounce bag frozen green peas, thawed,
  plus an additional 1½ to 2 cups frozen green peas,
  thawed, reserved
- 8 to 10 ounces spinach (any variety), stemmed,
  or a combination of spinach and arugula
- 1 head lettuce, any variety, coarsely chopped
- ½ bunch watercress leaves (some stems are fine)
- ¼ cup parsley leaves
- ¼ cup minced fresh dill
- 1 teaspoon curry powder

  Juice of 1 to 1½ lemons, to taste

  Salt and freshly ground pepper to taste

  Thinly sliced radishes and chopped radish tops
  for topping, optional

  Snipped chives for topping, optional

Heat the oil in a soup pot. Add the leeks and sauté until translucent. Add the garlic and continue to sauté until the leeks are tender and just beginning to turn golden.

Add the broth and bring to a gentle boil. Add the 16 ounce bag of peas and return to a gentle simmer. In batches, add the spinach and the arugula, if you're using it, then the lettuce, cooking only until they're wilted. Remove from the heat.

Stir in the watercress, parsley, half of the dill, curry powder, and lemon juice. Transfer to a food processor and puree in batches, then return to the soup pot. Or simply insert an immersion blender into the pot and puree until the soup is smooth.

Adjust the consistency to your liking with additional water. Stir in the reserved peas and remaining dill. Heat through as needed, season with salt and pepper, and serve.

Variation
For additional richness and body, add a medium-ripe avocado, peeled and coarsely chopped, before you puree.

Red Lentil Dal with Red Beans & Greens

6 or more servings

Dal, a cross between a hot dip and a soup made of well-cooked legumes, is meant to be scooped up with freshly made Indian breads, such as chapatis. If you can't find chapatis, try fresh pita bread or any other fresh flat bread you prefer. Tiny red lentils, available in natural food stores and imported food shops, cook to an appealing orange-gold color. Greens boost the visual and nutritional impact of this dish.

1	**tablespoon vegetable oil**
1	**medium onion, minced**
2	**cloves garlic, minced**
1	**cup dried red lentils, rinsed**
1	**to 2 teaspoons minced fresh or jarred ginger**
2	**teaspoons curry powder or garam masala**
1	**teaspoon ground cumin**
½	**teaspoon ground turmeric**
1	**15- to 16-ounce can kidney or red beans, rinsed**
8	**to 10 ounces tender small greens (choose 2 or 3 from among spinach, arugula, dandelion greens, or watercress, coarsely chopped)**
	Salt and freshly ground pepper to taste

Heat the oil in a large saucepan or small soup pot. Add the onion and garlic, and sauté over medium heat until golden.

Add the lentils, 3 cups water, and spices. Bring to a simmer, then cover and cook over low heat for 25 minutes, or until the lentils are quite mushy. The texture should be like a very thick soup. If need be, simmer uncovered until the mixture thickens up.

Stir in the beans, then add the greens in batches, stirring them in until they're just wilted. Season with salt and pepper and serve.

Leek & Potato Soup with Watercress

6 servings

The bright color and flavor of watercress adds a touch of spring to a simple classic soup. If you can make this the night before it's needed, so much the better, since the flavors improve from standing overnight.

1½   **tablespoons olive oil**

  3   **large leeks, white and palest green parts only, chopped and rinsed well**

  4   **large potatoes, peeled and diced**

  1   **bay leaf**

  2   **vegetable bouillon cubes**

  1   **cup packed watercress leaves**

  1   **to 1½ cups rice milk**

     Salt and freshly ground pepper to taste

 ¼   **cup chopped fresh parsley, more or less, to taste**

Heat the oil in a large soup pot. Add the leeks and sauté over medium heat, covered, until they just begin to turn golden. Stir occasionally.

Add the potatoes, bay leaf, bouillon cubes, and just enough water to cover. Bring to a simmer, then simmer gently, covered, until the potatoes are tender, about 15 to 20 minutes.

Mash some of the potatoes against the side of the pot with the back of a spoon and stir back into the soup to thicken it. Add the watercress and rice milk, and simmer over very low heat for 10 minutes longer. Season with salt and pepper.

Allow the soup to stand off the heat for an hour or two before serving, or let it cool and refrigerate overnight. Heat through before serving. Stir in the parsley. If needed, adjust the consistency with more rice milk, and adjust the seasonings.

Curried Spinach & Chickpea Soup

6 or more servings

Inspired by the classic compatibility of spinach and chickpeas, this soup is equally good with an array of other greens, as suggested in the variations below.

2   **tablespoons olive oil**

1   **medium onion, finely chopped**

2   **to 4 cloves garlic, minced**

2   **medium carrots, peeled and finely diced**

1   **large stalk celery, finely diced**

1   **14- to 16-ounce can diced tomatoes (try fire-roasted)**

2   **teaspoons curry powder**

¼   **teaspoon each: ground nutmeg, cinnamon, and coriander**

8   **ounces baby spinach leaves, rinsed**

1   **16-ounce can chickpeas, drained and rinsed**

    Salt and freshly ground pepper to taste

Heat the oil in a large soup pot. Add the onion, garlic, carrots, and celery, and sauté over medium heat until all are golden.

Add 6 cups water followed by the tomatoes and spices and bring to a slow boil. Cover and simmer gently for 15 to 20 minutes.

Stir the spinach and chickpeas into the soup and continue to simmer over very low heat for 5 minutes longer. Season with salt and pepper and serve.

Variations

Use baby arugula in place of the spinach, or part of it; or substitute any variety of chard or summer spinach, mustard greens, or escarole, leaves chopped and stems thinly sliced.

Quick Quinoa & Spring Greens Soup

6 servings

Perfect for a rainy spring evening, this light, greens-filled soup comes together in a snap as soon as the quinoa is cooked.

- ½ **cup quinoa, rinsed in a fine sieve**
- 1 **tablespoon olive oil**
- 3 **to 4 scallions, white and green parts, sliced**
- 2 **to 3 garlic scapes, cut into 1-inch sections (substitute 3 to 4 cloves minced garlic if scapes are not available)**
- 1 **32-ounce carton vegetable broth**
- 2 **tablespoons lemon juice**
- ½ **bunch watercress leaves**
- 2 **good handfuls baby spinach, arugula, tatsoi, or mizuna**
- 1 **handful cleaned, chopped radish greens**
- ¼ **cup chopped fresh parsley or cilantro**
- **Salt and freshly ground pepper to taste**
- 4 **to 6 radishes, thinly sliced**

Combine the quinoa with 1 cup water in a saucepan. Bring to a rapid simmer, then lower the heat, cover, and simmer gently until the water is absorbed, about 15 minutes.

Meanwhile, heat the oil in a small soup pot. Add the scallions and the garlic scapes and sauté over medium heat for 2 minutes.

Add the broth plus 2 cups water. Bring to a slow boil, then add the lemon juice, watercress, spinach or other greens, radish greens, and parsley. Simmer for just a minute or so, until the greens are wilted. Remove from the heat.

Stir in the cooked quinoa and season with salt and pepper. Serve at once, garnishing each serving with a few slices of radish.

Asian Noodle Soup
with Greens & Shiitake Mushrooms

4 to 6 servings

This simple soup is a good first course for a mixed vegetable and tofu stir-fry.

1   **4-ounce bundle bean-thread noodles**

1   **32-ounce carton vegetable broth**

4   **ounces fresh shiitake mushrooms, cleaned, stemmed, and thinly sliced**

4   **to 6 stalks regular bok choy, or 1 to 2 baby bok choy, with leaves, sliced**

6   **to 8 ounces Asian greens (Chinese broccoli, or any of the other choys), stalks cut into 1-inch segments, leaves sliced**

2   **to 3 scallions, white parts thinly sliced**

2   **tablespoons reduced-sodium soy sauce, or to taste**

   Freshly ground pepper to taste

Combine the bean-thread noodles with enough hot water to cover in a heatproof container. Let them soak, covered, until *al dente,* about 20 minutes or according to package directions. Drain well, then transfer the noodles to a cutting board and chop them in several directions to shorten.

Meanwhile, combine the vegetable broth with the shiitakes in a soup pot and bring to a simmer. Cover and simmer gently for 10 minutes.

Add the greens, scallions, and soy sauce, and simmer for 2 to 3 minutes more, just until the greens are wilted. Stir in the noodles and additional water, about 1 to 2 cups, then season to taste with freshly ground pepper, and serve at once.

Variations
Substitute tatsoi, mizuna, baby or regular spinach, watercress, mustard greens, napa cabbage, or any combination of these, if the choys are unavailable

Chinese Cabbage, Tofu & Mushroom Soup

4 to 6 servings

Here's an easy rendition of traditional Chinese cabbage and bean curd soup. Once the flavorful mushroom broth is ready, the rest of the soup comes together in a flash. In addition to the customary napa cabbage, this version calls for a splash of extra green from tatsoi or spinach.

FOR THE MUSHROOM BROTH:

- 1 small onion, finely chopped
- 2 cloves garlic, minced
- 8 to 10 dried shiitake mushrooms
- 2 tablespoons reduced-sodium soy sauce, or to taste
- ¼ cup dry wine or cooking sherry

- ½ head napa cabbage, cut into short ribbons
- 1 cup cremini or baby bella mushrooms, stemmed and thinly sliced
- 8 ounces soft or firm tofu, cut into ½-inch dice
- 2 big handfuls tatsoi or baby spinach
- 2 to 3 scallions, green part only, thinly sliced
- Salt and freshly ground pepper to taste

Combine ingredients for the mushroom broth in a small soup pot with 6 cups of water and bring to a slow boil. Lower the heat, then cover and simmer gently for 20 minutes. Scoop the mushrooms out with a slotted spoon. Cut away and discard the stems, and slice the caps; return them to the broth.

Add the napa cabbage and mushrooms to the broth; return to a gentle boil; then lower the heat, cover, and cook for 2 to 3 minutes, or until the cabbage and mushrooms have softened. Stir in the tofu, tatsoi or spinach, and scallions, and cook just until the greens are wilted.

Remove from the heat, season with salt and pepper, and serve at once.

Hot-&-Sour Vegetable Soup with Asian Greens

6 servings

I especially love hot-and-sour soup as a cold remedy, although it's good any time, particularly as a first course to an Asian-style meal. This variation cooks very quickly; if anything, err on the side of less cooking rather than more. Despite the long list of ingredients, once the veggies are prepped this soup is ready for the table in just a few minutes. If you'd like to use more greens than are called for here, by all means go ahead—the more, the better. If you add more greens, be sure to adjust the amount of water as well as the balance of hot and sour flavors.

1 tablespoon safflower or other healthy vegetable oil

3 to 4 cloves garlic, minced

1 32-ounce carton vegetable broth

1 to 1½ cups mushrooms, any variety, cleaned and sliced

2 cups small broccoli florets

½ medium red bell pepper, cut into short, narrow strips

2 medium ripe tomatoes, finely diced

1 15-ounce can baby corn, with liquid

¼ cup rice vinegar, or more, to taste

1 tablespoon natural granulated sugar

Thai red chili paste, cayenne pepper, or any hot sauce, to taste

2 or 3 stalks regular bok choy, or 1 baby bok choy, stems sliced diagonally, leaves chopped

8 ounces Asian greens, any variety (use one or two kinds; choose from among the choys, tatsoi, mizuna, and napa cabbage)

2 scallions, sliced

2 tablespoons cornstarch

Lots of freshly ground pepper

Reduced-sodium soy sauce to taste

Heat the oil in a soup pot. Add the garlic and sauté over low heat until golden.

Add the broth plus 1 cup water, the mushrooms, broccoli, bell pepper, tomatoes, and baby corn. Bring to a gentle boil, then add the vinegar and sugar; then lower the heat, cover, and simmer gently for 5 minutes, or until the vegetables are just tender.

If you choose to use chili paste as your "hot stuff," start with ½ teaspoon, dissolved in a little water. Cayenne or another hot sauce can be sprinkled in to taste.

Add the bok choy, greens, and scallions and simmer just until the greens are wilted

Dissolve the cornstarch in about ¼ cup water. Slowly drizzle into the soup while stirring. Adjust the consistency of the soup with a bit more water if it's too dense. Taste and adjust the hot-and-sour balance, then season with pepper and soy sauce. Remove from the heat and serve at once.

Miso Chinese Vegetable Soup with Corn & Leafy Greens

6 servings

Miso soups are particularly warming on chilly days, and this one is no exception. You don't often find an abundance of leafy greens in traditional miso soups, but their mellow flavor works quite well with salty miso. Like the other Asian-flavored soups presented in this chapter, this one comes together quickly.

1   **tablespoon olive oil or other healthy vegetable oil**

1   **medium onion, quartered and thinly sliced**

1   **medium carrot, thinly sliced**

2   **cloves garlic, minced**

2   **4- to 5-inch pieces wakame (sea vegetable), optional**

2   **cups fresh (from 2 medium ears) or frozen corn kernels**

1   **4- to 5-inch section of daikon radish,**
    or 1 medium turnip, peeled and diced

3   **to 4 scallions, white and green parts, thinly sliced**

¼   **cup dry red wine or sherry**

8   **ounces Asian greens, any variety (use one or two kinds;**
    choose from among the choys, tatsoi, and mizuna)

2   **cups snow peas, cut into 1-inch pieces**

8   **ounces soft or firm tofu, finely diced, optional**

3   **tablespoons miso, or more, to taste**

    Freshly ground pepper to taste

Heat the oil in a small soup pot. Add the onion, carrots, and garlic. Sauté over medium heat until all are golden.

Add 6 cups water followed by the wakame (if you are using it), corn, daikon radish or turnip, white parts of the scallion, and wine. Bring to a gentle boil and simmer until the corn and daikon radish or turnip, are just tender, not more than 3 minutes.

Stir in the greens, snow peas, tofu (if you are using it), and green parts of the scallion. Simmer for 2 minutes longer, then stir in the tofu (if you are using it). Remove from the heat.

Dissolve the miso in ½ cup warm water. Stir into the soup. Adjust the consistency of the soup with more water if the ingredients are too crowded, then taste and add more dissolved miso if you'd like. Season with pepper and serve at once.

CHAPTER 5

GREEN JUICES & SMOOTHIES

I asked myself what seemed a hypothetical question: When was the first time someone looked at kale and said, "Hmmm . . . how would that taste in a beverage"? As it turns out, there is an answer to this: Victoria Boutenko, who has done much to popularize the raw food movement, has often been credited with creating and developing the idea of green smoothies —a trend that is here to stay. Green juices are quite popular as well, but they involve a little extra work and cleanup. Whichever form you prefer, or if you like both, this chapter offers a brief introduction to making these amazing green drinks.

GREEN JUICES

Green "C" Monster Juice, 205

Greens, Cucumber & Apple Juice, 205

Beets & Greens Juice with Apple & Ginger, 206

Spinach & Lettuce Refresher, 206

Sparkling Spinach Juice, 207

GREEN SMOOTHIES

Green Velvet Smoothie with Banada & Avocado, 209

Spinach Piña Colada Smoothie, 210

Greens, Cucumber & Pineapple Smoothie, 210

Spinach & Mango or Peach Smoothie, 211

Greens & Apple Smoothie, 211

Burgundy Berry Bliss Smoothie, 212

Fall Harvest Green Smoothie, 212

Kale & Pear Smoothie, 213

Nutty Chocolate-Banana & Spinach Smoothie, 213

GREEN JUICES VS. GREEN SMOOTHIES

Making good green smoothies requires a high-speed blender. The two most popular brands are Vita-Mix and Blend'Tec, but there are other good high-speed blenders on the market. Comparison shop, of course, but know that in order to make a truly smooth green smoothie you need a good-quality high-speed blender—not an ordinary blender.

Smoothies are easier to prepare than juices because the cleanup is such a snap, and even though the whole leaf and accompanying fruit is used, the resulting beverage doesn't taste or feel like it's filled with fiber. On the other hand, the essence of a lot more greens and fruit can go into one serving of juice, making it a more potent source of nutrients and enzymes. In both cases, it's very important to use only organic produce. Smoothies and juices are both concentrated sources of produce, and you don't want to add pesticides to the mix.

From personal experience and that of a number of friends, I can tell you that the cleanup required after juicing can be a bit daunting—a point that seems to be the most common deal breaker in the juicer versus blender debate. A number of years ago I went gung-ho on a juicer; after a month or so I demoted it from the counter to the cabinet, and it rarely emerged after that. My Vita-Mix, on the other hand, has been on the counter for years, and rarely a day goes by when it's not used for one thing or another.

Despite the fact that I love freshly pressed juices, especially green ones, I didn't want to invest in another machine that would likely go the way of the first one, so I enlisted my younger son, Evan, who was making wonderful concoctions at a local vegan café while I was writing this book, to help me develop some recipes that would be both relatively easy to make and delicious to drink. I thank him—and Seth Branitz and Jenn Liemer Branitz of Karma Road Organic Vegan Deli (karmaroad.net) in New Paltz, New York, who provided the space and machinery—for developing these recipes.

THE BENEFITS OF SMOOTHIES

Contributed by Nathalie Lussier

1. Smoothies keep longer in the refrigerator than juices. Smoothies contain all the fiber that the fruits and vegetables initially come with, albeit in a blended form. Because everything is still in the drink itself, you can actually store smoothies longer than juices without losing too much nutritional value. To preserve a smoothie you simply need to put it in a glass container such as a mason jar and fill it to the brim. Because this keeps the air out, the smoothie will not oxidize. Seal the jar and drink it within 24 to 32 hours. You might need to shake it if the liquid separates.

2. The fiber in a green smoothie acts like a chimney sweeper. Since smoothies still contain all the fiber from fruits and vegetables, they have a cleansing effect on the bowel.

3. Sugar is absorbed slowly because of the built-in fiber. Green smoothies allow you to enjoy all the benefits of fruit without experiencing sugar spiking and the ensuing crash. The fiber regulates the flow of sugar into the bloodstream as your body digests it.

4. Blenders are easy to clean. A blender can easily be cleaned by running it under the tap or adding a bit of water and soap to it and pushing the clean-cycle button for a few seconds. Because blenders are so easy to assemble and clean, a lot of people gravitate toward blending instead of juicing.

5. Fruit smoothies are great tasting for the whole family. Green smoothies work well because you can mix and match a little extra fruit, or maybe a spoonful of cacao, to please the taste buds of anyone in your household.

6. You can easily add supplements and superfoods to smoothies. When making a smoothie, you can add a spoonful of hemp protein powder, spirulina, or maca root powder, for example, to give yourself a nutritional edge. You wouldn't necessarily want to add these supplements to a glass of juice because of their effect on the taste or texture of the juice.

THE BENEFITS OF JUICING

Contributed by Nathalie Lussier

1. Fresh juices are a shortcut to pure nutrition. A freshly made juice bypasses the need to digest the fibers before you get all the nutrients of the fruits and vegetables. This is ideal for people who have digestion problems and need to heal themselves before they can absorb nutrients from whole foods.

2. Juice vegetables, but eat fruits. Vegetables are better juiced, whereas fruits are better eaten whole. Fruits need all of the fiber in order to slow down the absorption of sugar in your bloodstream. (The exception is mixing apple juice with vegetables.) Vegetables contain less sugar than fruit and therefore don't need as much fiber to slow down the absorption of sugar.

3. Juice gives you an instant energy boost. When you're drinking freshly made juice, you're getting all of the energy right away without waiting for your body to digest it. This has an immediately emerging effect.

4. Even without all of the fiber contained in smoothies, juices are a great way to flush out your system and to cleanse your body.

5. Juices don't make you feel as full as a smoothie. Drinking juice adds more nutrition to your day without making you feel as if you've just eaten a whole meal. After drinking juice you might be satisfied for 30 minutes to an hour. After drinking a smoothie, you might be satisfied for two to three hours.

6. You can juice almost any fruit or vegetable. You may not put a beet or a carrot in one of your smoothies, but you can definitely make juice out of these ingredients. Interestingly enough, you can disguise the taste of some vegetables with other vegetables and apples and make a juice that also contains a greater variety of ingredients and nutrients. This isn't always the case with smoothies.

GREEN JUICES

Green "C" Monster Juice

About two 12-ounce servings

In this recipe, a few good sources of vitamin C add up to one great C-filled juice—with plenty of great flavor as well as nutrition.

- 2 **to 3 carrots, cleaned and cut into chunks**
- 2 **big handfuls spinach leaves (any variety),**
  or 3 to 4 kale leaves or beet greens, coarsely chopped
- ½ **medium red beet**
- 1 **1-inch piece ginger**
- 2 **to 3 oranges**
  Lemon juice to taste

Juice the first four ingredients and divide them between two tumblers. Juice the oranges with a citrus juicer and add lemon juice to your liking.

Greens, Cucumber & Apple Juice

Two servings, about 12 ounces each

The inspiration for this juice recipe comes from Karma Road, an incredible little vegan café (with a big heart) in New Paltz, New York.

- 3 **to 4 kale leaves, torn**
- 2 **big handfuls spinach leaves (any variety)**
- 1 **medium cucumber, cut into chunks**
- 2 **to 3 medium apples, cored and cut into chunks**
- ½ **to 1 lemon, to taste**

Juice the first four ingredients and divide between two tumblers. Juice the lemon with a citrus juicer and add lemon juice to your liking to the green juice.

Beets & Greens Juice with Apple & Ginger

About two 8-ounce servings

I just adore beet juice. Apples provide just the right amount of sweetness, and the addition of the beet greens supercharges the results.

1   **medium beet, washed well, bruised spots cut away**

Greens from 3 to 4 beets

3   **medium apples**

Handful of parsley leaves

1   **1-inch piece ginger**

½   **to 1 lemon, to taste**

Juice the first five ingredients and divide between two tumblers. Juice the lemon with a citrus juicer and add lemon juice to your liking.

Spinach & Lettuce Refresher

About two 8-ounce servings

Served over ice, this hydrating juice is wonderful in warm weather.

2   **big handfuls spinach leaves (any variety)**

4   **leaves romaine lettuce**

2   **medium apples**

½   **medium cucumber**

Handful of parsley leaves

½   **lemon or lime**

Agave nectar to taste

Juice the first five ingredients and divide between two tumblers. Juice the lemon or lime with a citrus juicer and add lemon or lime juice and agave nectar to your liking.

Sparkling Spinach Juice

Two 12-ounce servings

The ingredients in this mix add up to a delightfully refreshing green "soda."

- **1 medium cucumber, cut into chunks**
- **1 celery stalk, cut into chunks**
- **2 big handfuls spinach leaves**
-    **Handful of parsley leaves, optional**
- **1 lemon or lime**
-    **Seltzer, as needed**
-    **Agave nectar to taste**

Juice the first three ingredients (plus the parsley, if you're using it) and divide between two tumblers.

Juice the lemon or lime with a citrus juicer and divide between the two tumblers. Fill the tumblers with seltzer (leaving a little room for ice if desired), then sweeten with agave nectar. Serve at once at room temperature or over ice.

GREEN SMOOTHIES BASICS

Some green-smoothie advocates recommend making these beverages with nothing but fruit, greens, and water for maximum digestibility. Others like to use juice or a nondairy milk rather than water, for more flavor and substance. Other common additions are protein powder and omega-rich seeds like hemp, flax, or chia. The nice thing about green smoothies is that there's no wrong way to make them, and once you've experimented with a few combinations, you'll discover your own favorites. You might like thick smoothies, in which case banana is a good addition, or if you like a juicier smoothie, cucumber is a good addition. Feel free to alter and experiment with the recipes that follow and come up with your own variations.

I've learned that green smoothies should be about 60 percent fruit and 40 percent greens. It isn't always possible to measure precisely, though it's fairly evident that a somewhat larger ratio of fruit makes the smoothie sweeter and smoother. It's also good to vary the kind of greens you use in your smoothies, especially if you get into the habit of making them daily. Spinach, kale, and collards have the best flavors for blending into smoothies. In fact, spinach is so mild that if you close your eyes and just taste, you hardly know it's there. Most people prefer milder greens in smoothies over more bitter or sharp varieties, but if you have a notion that you'd like mustard greens in your smoothie, by all means, give it a whirl—both literally and figuratively!

If you'd like your green smoothies less green, simply reduce the amount of greens called for. You can also experiment with other fruits and nutritional embellishments such as protein powder. On the other hand, if you think greener is better, use more greens! Also note that some green-smoothie advocates prefer using filtered water as the liquid rather than the juices or nondairy milks I call for in the recipes in this section. I like the added flavor and body provided by liquids other than water, but experiment to see if water is what you prefer.

I haven't included the entire gamut of what can go into smoothies (or juices, for that matter) in this brief chapter, so feel free to experiment with other produce (like grapes, watermelon, and celery) to create beverages that will boost your vitality and make you feel clean and radiant.

Green Velvet Smoothie with Banana & Avocado

Two 12-ounce servings

Hemp seeds are one of the best, most concentrated sources of omega-3s—better (and tastier) than flaxseeds. They make a great addition to this creamy smoothie. You can find hemp seeds and hemp milk at most natural foods markets.

- 2 **medium curly kale or collard leaves, torn**
- 1 **medium banana, peeled and cut into chunks**
- ½ **medium ripe avocado, peeled and cut into chunks**
- 2 **cups vanilla nondairy milk (try almond or hemp milk)**
- 2 **tablespoons hemp seeds, optional (but highly recommended)**

  Lemon juice to taste

  Agave nectar to taste

Combine the greens, banana, avocado, nondairy milk, and hemp seeds (if you're using them) in a blender. Blend on high speed until completely smooth.

Pour into a 12-ounce tumbler and add a little lemon juice and agave nectar to taste. Drink at once at room temperature or add an ice cube or two.

Spinach Piña Colada Smoothie

Two servings, about 12 ounces each

Spinach and pineapple are a companionable pairing, and a double dose of coconut makes this drink quite luscious tasting, but not high in fat. Coconut water has an abundance of electrolytes, which aid in hydration, especially after physical exertion.

1   **10- to 12-ounce container coconut water**

1   **cup diced fresh or canned pineapple**

1   **to 2 generous handfuls baby spinach leaves, rinsed**

1   **6-ounce container vanilla coconut yogurt**

2   **tablespoons hemp seeds, optional**

Combine all the ingredients in a blender and process until quite smooth. Divide between two tumblers and serve at once. Serve over ice if you like.

Greens, Cucumber & Pineapple Smoothie

Two servings, about 12 ounces each

This incredibly refreshing and hydrating smoothie is one of my favorites.

1   **cup diced fresh or canned pineapple**

½   **medium or 1 small sweet apple, cored and cut into chunks**

1   **4-inch piece cucumber (leave peel on if unwaxed)**

2   **to 3 medium kale or collard leaves, coarsely chopped**

2   **tablespoons hemp seeds or chia seeds, optional**

1   **cup mango or pineapple juice, or coconut water**

Combine all the ingredients in a high-speed blender and process until quite smooth. Divide between two tumblers. If the smoothies are too thick, stir in a bit more juice, then serve at once.

Spinach & Mango or Peach Smoothie

Two servings, about 12 ounces each

Mango gives green smoothies a tropical twist. If your mango is a bit stringy, a high-speed blender will smooth it out.

- 1 **cup mango chunks (fresh or frozen)**
- ½ **medium banana, peeled and cut into chunks**
- 1 **cup vanilla nondairy milk**
- 2 **big handfuls spinach leaves**
- 1 **teaspoon vanilla extract**

Combine all the ingredients in a high-speed blender and process until quite smooth. Divide between two tumblers and serve at once.

Greens & Apple Smoothie

Two 12-ounce or three 8-ounce servings

This smoothie is my go-to formula. I use cucumber when I want a lighter, juicier effect, and add a banana when the weather calls for something comforting.

- 2 **big handfuls baby spinach, or 2 medium curly kale or collard leaves**
- 1 **medium apple, cored and cut into large chunks**
- 1 **3- to 4-inch piece cucumber, preferably peeled and cut into chunks, or ½ large banana**
- 1 **cup vanilla nondairy milk or fruit juice, or ½ cup each**
- 1 **to 2 tablespoons hemp seeds or chia seeds, optional**
- 2 **teaspoons agave nectar or other liquid sweetener, optional**
- 2 **tablespoons lemon juice**

Combine all the ingredients in a blender. Process until completely smooth. Divide between two or three tumblers and serve at once.

Burgundy Berry Bliss Smoothie

Two 12-ounce servings or three 8-ounce servings

Combining blueberries, raspberries, or strawberries and greens results in a burgundy beverage that's as tasty as it is pretty. If you're not using any frozen ingredients in this smoothie, you may want to serve it over a couple of ice cubes.

½ **cup blueberries (fresh or frozen)**

½ **cup raspberries or strawberries (fresh or frozen)**

1 **small banana, or ½ large banana (pre-frozen if desired)**

1 **large collard green leaf, or 2 medium curly kale leaves**

1 **cup berry juice, such as pomegranate**

1 **cup vanilla nondairy milk**

Combine all the ingredients in a high-speed blender. Process until completely smooth. Serve at once.

Fall Harvest Green Smoothie

Two 12-ounce servings or three 8-ounce servings

Here's an offbeat smoothie that takes advantage of autumn ingredients. A high-speed blender makes quick work of raw squash, but if you have any leftover baked squash, it will work just as well.

2 **medium collard or curly kale green leaves**

1 **medium apple or pear, cored and coarsely chopped**

½ **cup peeled and diced raw or baked butternut squash**

2 **tablespoons hemp or flaxseeds, optional**

1 **cup pear nectar or apple cider**

½ **cup vanilla nondairy milk**

A pinch each of cinnamon and nutmeg

Combine all the ingredients in a high-speed blender. Process until completely smooth. Serve at once.

Kale & Pear Smoothie

Two servings, about 12 ounces each

If you like pears, you'll love this smoothie, with its double dose of this mellow fruit. If you like the flavor of fresh mint, add a few leaves for a nice finishing touch.

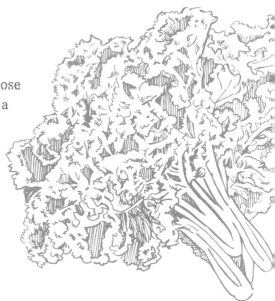

- 2 **medium ripe pears, cored and chopped**
- 3 **to 4 curly kale leaves**
- ½ **medium banana, optional**
- 2 **tablespoons hemp or flaxseeds, optional**
- 1 **cup pear nectar**
- ½ **cup vanilla nondairy milk**
   Several mint leaves, optional

Combine all the ingredients in a high-speed blender and process until quite smooth. Divide between two tumblers. If the smoothies are too thick, stir in a bit more juice, then serve at once.

Nutty Chocolate-Banana & Spinach Smoothie

Two 12-ounce servings

This rich smoothie is a good way to woo green-smoothie skeptics. The spinach blends beautifully into the chocolaty backdrop.

- 1 **medium banana, peeled and cut into chunks (frozen, if desired)**
- 1½ **cups chocolate nondairy milk**
- 1 **to 2 handfuls spinach leaves**
- 2 **tablespoons peanut, cashew, or almond butter**
- 2 **tablespoon hemp, flax, or chia seeds, optional**

Combine all the ingredients in a regular blender—or a high-speed blender if you want to include the seeds—and process until smoothly pureed. Divide between two tumblers and serve at once.

METRIC CONVERSIONS

Get metric equivalents for volume, temperatures, and weights for all of your most commonly used cooking and baking measurements right here.

Volume

US	METRIC
1 teaspoon	5 ml
1 tablespoon	15 ml
¼ cup	60 ml
⅓ cup	80 ml
⅔ cup	160 ml
¾ cups	180 ml
1 cup	240 ml
1 pint	475 ml
1 quart	.95 liter
1 quart plus ¼ cup	1 liter
1 gallon	3.8 liters

Temperature

To convert from Fahrenheit to Celsius: subtract 32, multiply by 5, then divide by 9

32° F	0° C
212° F	100° C
250° F	121° C
325° F	163° C
350° F	176° C
375° F	190° C
400° F	205° C
425° F	218° C
450° F	232° C

Weight

US	METRIC
1 ounce	28.3 grams
4 ounces	113 grams
8 ounces	227 grams
12 ounces	340.2 grams

Excerpted from *The Good Housekeeping Cookbook* (Hearst Books/Sterling Publishing).

INDEX

ABOUT THE AUTHOR

Nava Atlas is the author and illustrator of many well-known vegetarian and vegan cookbooks, including *Vegan Holiday Kitchen, Vegan Express, Vegan Soups and Hearty Stews for All Seasons, The Vegetarian Family Cookbook,* and *The Vegetarian 5-Ingredient Gourmet.* Her first book was *Vegetariana,* now considered a classic in its field. In addition, she has published two books of humor, *Expect the Unexpected When You're Expecting!* and *Secret Recipes for the Modern Wife.* Her most recent book of visual nonfiction is *The Literary Ladies' Guide to the Writing Life.*

Nava is also a visual artist, specializing in limited-edition artist's books and text-driven objects and installations. Her work has been shown nationally in museums, galleries, and alternative art spaces. Her limited-edition books are housed in numerous collections of artist's books, including the art libraries at the Museum of Modern Art (NY), the National Museum of Women in the Arts (Washington, DC), the Victoria and Albert Museum (London), the Brooklyn Museum, and the Boston Museum of Fine Arts, as well as dozens of academic collections.

To learn more about Nava's work visit her various Web sites: VegKitchen.com, navaatlasart.com, and literaryladiesguide.com. Nava has two grown sons and lives in the Hudson Valley region of New York State with her husband.

ABOUT THE PHOTOGRAPHER

Susan Voisin writes and photographs the popular blog *FatFree Vegan Kitchen* (blog.fatfreevegan.com), which was given the Readers' Choice award by *VegNews* magazine in 2007, 2009, 2010, and 2011. She received the WellFed Network's Food Blog Award for Best Theme in 2007.